Life for Dry Bones

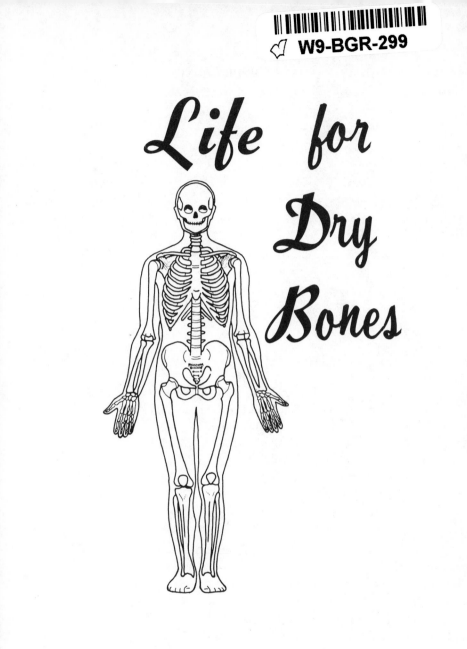

Pulpit Messages for the First 13 Sundays after Pentecost

Louis H. Valbracht, D. D.

LIFE FOR DRY BONES

.

PRINTED IN U.S.A.

TABLE OF CONTENTS

Preface 3
The Day of Pentecost......................... 5
    So You're Only Human
The Holy Trinity (First Sunday after Pentecost)... 16
    The Priesthood of Parents
Second Sunday after Pentecost 26
    Handling the Future
Third Sunday after Pentecost 34
    The Seen and Unseen
Fourth Sunday after Pentecost 42
    He Knows Not How
Fifth Sunday after Pentecost 52
    Why Are You Afraid?
Sixth Sunday after Pentecost.................. 62
    When Your Mouth's in the Dust
St. James the Elder, Apostle 71
    The Lonesome Road
Eighth Sunday after Pentecost 80
    The Faith of the Foolish
Ninth Sunday after Pentecost 88
    The Fence Builders
Mary, Mother of Our Lord 96
    She Didn't Understand
Eleventh Sunday after Pentecost 103
    So You're Mad at God?
Twelfth Sunday after Pentecost 111
    Want to Imitate God?

To my parents, The Rev. Dr. and Mrs.
Edward F. Valbracht, who through his
preaching and teaching and her unquench-
able love brought life to my dry bones.

L.H.V.

PREFACE

My title, "Life for Dry Bones," is taken from the Old Testament Lesson for Pentecost of Series B in the three-year Lectionary. The question comes to Ezekiel from the Lord: " 'Son of man, can these bones live?' And I answered, 'O Lord God, thou knowest.' Again he said to me, 'Prophesy to these bones, and say to them, O dry bones, hear the word of the Lord. Thus says the Lord God to these bones: Behold, I will cause breath to enter you, and you shall live.' " Of course, the reference is from that piercing part of Ezekiel's vision in which he walks through the valley of dry bones, and the assurance of the Lord is that by His Holy Spirit, these dry bones may have live. That, of course, is its obvious connection with the Pentecost.

To me, however, the text suggests much more. The Gospel read as the cold history of the ministry of Jesus Christ is but a heap of dry bones. Biblical study that produces only theology is dry bones. Theology that arrives only at doctrine or dogma is, again, but dry bones. A Christian Confession or Creed, without pragmatic expression in life, is dry bones. And the members of the Church, unendowed, unimproved, and uninspired by God's Holy Spirit, are tragically only another valley of dry bones. Indeed, the humanity of the world, God's family on earth, without His Spirit are all but dry bones, and the earth becomes a dead valley filled with them, unrelated, disconnected, useless, and dead.

Pentecost and the Post-Pentecost Season or the non-festival half of the Church Year is designed to take the living Word and make His Living Gospel bring life to the valley of dry bones in our life in contemporary, secular, Godless society.

In choosing the sermons for these Sundays, I have endeavored to pick the Lesson, Epistle, or Gospel which seems to relate itself most directly and powerfully to this task.

Someone once asked one of the great preachers of the last century: "Do the dead live:" He snapped back: "I can answer that without any question. The dead do live. All you have to do is visit one of my deacons' meetings to see proof of it."

There is many a preacher who looks over his congregation as he preaches and finds himself suddenly walking with Ezekiel and asking of the Lord the question that the Lord asked of Ezekiel: "Son of man, can these bones live?" And I am certain that many of us are extremely skeptical of that possibility. And yet, through the power of the Spirit, the Lord God says: "And I will lay sinews upon you, and will cause flesh to come upon you, and cover you with skin, and put breath in you, and you shall live; and you shall know that I am the Lord."

This is my prayer for all of us and to those who listen to the sound of our voices which have nothing to give but the Life that can come through the Spirit.

Louis H. Valbracht
Lententide, 1975

So You're Only Human

"Thus says the Lord God to these bones: behold, I will cause breath to enter you, and you shall live. And I will lay sinews upon you, and will cause flesh to come upon you, and cover you with skin, and put breath in you, and you shall live; and you shall know that I am the Lord."
(Ezekiel 37:5 and 6 RSV)

*****

A young woman came to me and told how she had borne a child out of wedlock. I asked her how she had gotten herself involved in such a situation. She said: "Well, I was away from home, working here in the city, and I was very lonely. And when this man became interested in me, I wasn't lonely anymore, and, well, I'm only human."

One of our young boys was apprehended while shoplifting in one of our department stores. I was called in to talk to him. I asked him what had prompted this kind of thievery, and he said: "Well, a lot of kids do it, and they get a lot of things. And so, I guess I'm only human, too."

I talked to a man who had been unfaithful to his wife

with her young sister who lived with them. He gave me this explanation: "She was always flirting with me, and one night when my wife was away, she made it perfectly obvious that she wanted me to make love to her, and, after all, I'm only human."

Why is it that when we disgrace ourselves, we promptly drag in this old cliche, this time-worn rationalization: "I'm only human." What do we mean "ONLY human?" Why the disparagement? Why does this, supposedly, explain our immorality? All right, so you're only human. What do you think that makes you? Who are you? What are your potentials? Because you are human, what are you supposed to be? Do you have any idea?

I remember the day I entered my first philosophy class in college, and the great old scholar who taught the course went through the usual procedure of calling the roll, having each one of us rise and be recognized when our name was called. That completed, he closed his class book, looked over his spectacles at us, and said with great emphasis: "We have spent approximately five minutes deciding WHO you are. We will now spend the rest of the semester deciding WHY you are, because this is the purpose of all religion, all philosophy, and all metaphysics."

The shortest poem in the world is "Why I?" and the attempt to answer that question has demanded the greatest and most profound thought of all mankind throughout the ages. In simple terms, if we have not asked and answered the query: "Why I" we actually have no business going on with this process that we call living.

Some months ago, I sought to cash a check in a distant city, and I was asked the usual question: "Do you have any identification?" Well, I found that I had about thirteen different kinds of identification, everything from my driver's license to my military I.D., to my Social Security card, to my "International Association of Turtles" membership card. And then, I was terribly tempted, as I often am, to ask in return: "You have asked me for identification. That is your duty. Now I ask YOU for your justification, motivation, aspiration. That is MY duty. You asked me WHO I am, and now I ask you WHY you are. Why are you living? What is your destiny?" But then, I know, I would have been creating a false dichotomy, just as the philosophy professor had, in essence, created one.

May I illustrate? One evening years ago, about dusk, along the shores of Lake Michigan in Chicago, I stopped my car just to enjoy the view and to spend a few minutes in quiet meditation and thought. Apparently, unwittingly, I had stumbled into a favorite Lovers' Lane. Well, very quickly a police officer was shining a flashlight in my face and asking, quite properly, the relevant questions. Both the philosopher and the bank teller, you see, were wrong. One had asked: "WHY are you?" and the other had asked "WHO are you?" but both of them had requested incomplete information. But, apparently, the policeman was a theologian. He linked the questions, as they must always be tied together, because on the answer of one depends the answer of the other, and he put the questions as each of us must answer them, if we are to make any sense at all out of human existence. He asked, quite politely: "Who are you, please, and what are you doing here?"

And so, I must ask you: "Who are you, please, and what are you doing here?"

In our text, Ezekiel looked out over the valley of dry bones, and he was seeing men worthless, useless, purposeless, and it was the Lord God who assured him that through His Spirit, those bones could live. We often ask the question: "Is there life after death?" Now we must answer what is, in actuality, the prior question: "Is there life after birth?" For many, the proper questions have not been answered, and so there is not life after birth. About one hundred people will commit suicide today in the United States. Do you remember Sutton

Vane's play, "Outward Bound?" A ship was moving out to sea, filled with people who had killed themselves, and the key line of the play was: "We are the people who should have had more courage." But I feel that Vane, the author of the play, missed the point completely. People do not kill themselves because of lack of courage, but because of lack of MEANING. In some cases, we might say that they are courageously acting out their answers to our questions. Who am I? Nobody that matters. What am I doing here? Nothing that makes any sense. Dry bones!

Every time I look at my Commission in the Navy, I think of the end of the life of the man who signed that Commission, the millionaire banker and one-time Secretary of the Navy, James Forrestal. His crushed body was found beside the wall of a hospital. In a room sixteen stories above, they found a slip of paper on which he had written some words. He had copied those words from the ancient poet, Sophocles, in his "Chorus from Ajax:"

> "Worn by the waste of time
> Comfortless, nameless, hopeless, save,
> In the dark prospect of the yawning grave."

And a book in the room lay open to these other words:

> "When reason's day sets rayless, joyless,
> Quenched in cold decay,
> Better to die and sleep,
> And never waking sleep
> Than linger on and dare to live
> When the soul's life has died."

You see? Comfortless, nameless, hopeless -- better to die than to live after the purpose of living is gone. James Forrestal had acted with cold logic on the basis of what he believed. It was his answer to: "Who are you?" and "What are you doing here?" If those who answered those questions in the SAME way acted upon them with the SAME cold precision that he did, then we would have a million suicides a day, rather than a hundred. There are truly legions of humans for whom there is no life after birth.

Who am I? Here are some of the answers from contemporary writers and philosophers: "Man is a thin layer of organic scum, which, for a short time, is coating the surface of one of our smaller planets." "Man is a pink froth, which the waves of evolution have washed up upon the shores of time." "Man is the only animal who can be a fool." Or Mark Twain said: "All I care to know is that man is a human being -- that is enough for me; it couldn't be worse." Or Nietzsche said: "Earth has a skin, and that skin has diseases, and one of those diseases is man."

How do we arrive at such answers? Dean Inge has called ours the "Century of Disappointment." Why the disappointment? Peter Marshall once prayed before the Senate: "God, give us strength to stand for something, lest we fall for everything." Well, we have fallen for a lot of things -- the gadgetry of materialism, for one thing. The naive believe that all we had to do was go on contriving gadgets and, ultimately, they would give meaning to life. By surrounding ourselves with the products of our technological skills, we would finally discover who we were. The automatic can opener, or the automatic garage door opener automatically, supposedly, open to us a new reason for living. We are told that a Buick Skylark is "something to believe in." How's that for naivete? How's that for gullibility? How's that for falling for everything?

One discerning editor put it this way: "An ostrich in a London zoo died the other day after eating a lunch of spikes, coins, tacks, a bullet, golf ball, knife handle, bottle stopper, spoon and can opener. The lack of protein will get anyone in time." And so we have gorged ourselves on gadgets and starved ourselves on the life-giving proteins of identity and meaning. We confuse the junk to live WITH with something to live FOR. We know HOW to do almost anything, but we've lost track of WHY we do anything that we do.

We have fallen for secularism, which holds that life on this earth is the boundary of all that man can, or needs to know. Secularism, of course, gives room for a variety of creeds. It has accommodated many philosophies in the last hundred years. Do you want a review? POSITIV- ISM, limiting knowledge to the scientifically verifiable experience. The only thing that we ever know is what we learn through scientifically verifiable processes. EMPIRICISM, whose ultimate standard is the report of our senses. I only know what I can feel or see or taste or hear. PRAGMATISM, whose test is: what is truth is whatever works. That's brilliant, isn't it? AGNOSTI- CISM, of the kind professed by Herbert Spencer who tripped himself up logically by holding that his only knowledge was that he had no knowledge, and that's about as logical as most agnostics, hypocritical as most of them are. They say: "I don't have enough knowledge to make a judgment," but they apparently had enough knowledge to make the judgment that they didn't have enough knowledge. And so, they're hypocrites. It included behaviorism, explaining all of our highest aspirations in convenient, mechanistic terms, until finally a lot of sensible people realized that a thinking behaviorist -- A THINKING BEHAVIORIST -- was a contradiction to his own theory, something that he'd never figured out for himself. The general mechanistic view of science, which the best scientists have now shot full of holes, is that if all our actions and attitudes were mechanistic, then we couldn't have decided what we already decided about it.

Oh, we fell for existentialism, which holds that life is essentially absurd, and we ignored the obvious contradiction that if life IS senseless, then our estimate of it as senseless is also senseless. The DETERMINIST who still prattles about progress, after saying that man is merely reacting to stimuli, and if the evolution of man is only an unplanned accident, then how can we assume that there IS any progress? And despite all of this prattle, toward what goal is this so-called progress progressing?

Montaigne wisely notes that the man who sums up his philosophy of life by saying that all of man's life and wisdom and fame is pure senselessness and vanity still wants his name on the front of the book to indicate that these were HIS thoughts, and he WANTS to have the fame that he says within the book he despises. The philosopher who says that man is of no importance, still wants to be considered important for saying it. So there it is, a short course in modern philosophy. How do you like it? And THIS is passed off as intelligence, the searching for relevance, for identity and meaning -- all of this intellectual gibberish, contradictions and stupidity. College sophomores taking their first course in philosophy are quite impressed by it. Some actually believe it, and they go through great motions of discussing it together seriously.

And so you have the stupid contradictions of men who would put man on this plane. Out of this kind of nonsense, we can truly say: "Well, we're only human."

On an ancient Roman tomb are the Latin words: "Non fui, fui, non sum, non curo," which is translated: "I was not, I was, I am not, I do not care." That's the summary of a life, and thank God that by His grace, we may think of ourselves more highly than the pagan or some of our modern pagans.

The psalmist 3000 years ago catches the vision: "When I consider the work of thy hands, the moon and the stars which thou hast ordained, what is man that thou art mindful of him?" And then he answers his own question: "Thou hast made him a little lower than divine."

John, in the New Testament, caught the full vision, the eternal dimension of man, as he says: "We are the sons of God." What an astonishing statement? Our lungs breathe the same air as the chimpanzee, but there is another breath in us -- God breathed into us, not the breath of life, but the breath of HIS life.

A Christian philosopher says: "Man is the only creature who says: 'I am, I ought, I can, I will.' " Consider: "I AM" -- man is capable of thought and introspection. He is the only creature who stands outside of himself and looks at himself to seek his own meaning. He is conscious of himself as a part of society. Descartes, the father of modern philosophy said: "I think" -- I THINK -- "therefore, I am. I am conscious of myself; therefore, I must have some significance to myself." I OUGHT -- what the philosophers call that categorical divine imperative, that thrust in man. I OUGHT -- that inherent sense of the moral law which God has created in each one of us. It has, for instance, driven us here to worship. What else? What else, except our sense of responsibility to Him? I CAN -- I have the opportunity of conscious choice. I WILL -- I have the freedom of will to do what I ought.

Why am I here? What am I doing here? I like the simple and profound words of the Westminster Catechism: "To serve God and enjoy Him forever." What rich relevance we find in those words: "To serve God and enjoy Him forever."

If any one of you has any other good reason that is rationally supportable and able to be documented logically, I welcome you to this pulpit to tell us about it, if you have one other logical reason for your being here. In all of my life, I have not yet heard one.

Recently one truly great scientist was invited to have his pedigree published in "Who's Who" and they sent him the usual blanks for him to fill out. One of the questions asked was: "Please list your chief titles and honors." The blank came back with this list:

"I am a
Child of the Creator
Temple of the Holy Spirit
Image of God
Redeemed Disciple of Christ

Working Member of His Kingdom
Member of the Fellowship of Saints
Candidate for Eternal life."

Quite high honors, aren't they? Oh, don't you ever dare say: "I'm ONLY human." You have the possibility of all of these honors and titles. Could there be anything higher?

The Priesthood of Parents

"And these words which I command you this day shall be upon your heart; and you shall teach them diligently to your children, and shall talk of them when you sit in your house, and when you walk by the way, and when you lie down, and when you rise. And you shall bind them as a sign upon your hand, and they shall be as frontlets between your eyes."

(Deuteronomy 6:6-8 RSV)

*****

Not long ago a fifteen-year-old boy came to me with what was, to him, a very serious moral problem. I assured him that his instinctive suspicion about the thing that his crowd of friends was doing -- that is, engaging in what they called "shoplifting contests," all going into different stores and seeing how much worth they could steal while they were in those stores -- that certainly was absolutely morally and legally wrong, and it was dangerous. But, most of all, it was contributing to a moral climate in which HE, as an adult, would have to live, one in which everyone would have to take it for granted that everyone else was a thief -- and there are such cultures in the world, as you know -- and that is not the kind of society that he and his friends, or anyone else, would want to live in. But then I asked him out of curiosity: "Why did you come to me? Certainly you could have talked this over with your parents, and they could have set you right on it. They could have given you the proper answers." And it was heartbreaking to see that lad's lips curl into a sneer, as he blurted out: "MY PARENTS? How could I ask them? They don't know what's right or wrong themselves. At least I've never seen any evidence of it."

Well, there it is. That's the problem we face. And may I quickly add that if, because of the subject of this sermon, you are not a parent because you're unmarried, or a childless couple, or your children are all grown up and gone from the home, you think this is not addressed to you, FORGET IT, because I am a preacher of the Gospel speaking from the atmosphere of Biblical custom and thought, and the attitude of the great civilizations who have gone before us, and still exist, that every man and woman adult is father or mother to EVERY child in that community, that clan, that tribe, or that nation. So, if you are eighteen years of age or over, this is addressed personally and directly to YOU, because YOU are the parents to countless children.

And so as Moses delivers the Law of the Covenant to the children of Israel, he makes it very clear that that Law must travel from parents to children, from generation to generation: "And these words which I command you this day shall be upon your heart, and you shall teach them diligently to your children and shall talk of them when you sit in your house and when you walk by the way and when you lie down and when you rise." That, truly, sets forth the obligation of all of the adults of a people to the children who come under their influence, and especially to the parents of the young. Their religious education will be a day-in day-out process from the beginning to the end of each day.

How many of us, when the obstetrical nurse placed that tiny bundle of humanity in our arms, realized that suddenly we had become a PRIEST OF GOD to that child? How many of us stopped long enough in congratulating ourselves that we had produced an offspring to realize that Almighty God, through NO POWER of ours whatsoever, had placed in our hands His most precious creation, a human life. That child, though born to us, or given to us as a child by adoption, would NEVER be ours -- WOULD NEVER BE OURS! It was forever God's son or daughter. We, as with all of God's gifts, were only the temporary stewards of that which comes from Him and BELONGS to Him eternally.

But with a child, we are more than just stewards, WE ARE PRIESTS! What is a priest? One who is an intermediary between God and man. Yes, we as Lutherans were the first to espouse the doctrine of the Universal Priesthood of All Believers, but nowhere does this priesthood become more evident than in our responsibility as parents. Indeed, psychologically, they tell us that the child's first god is its father. That's quite a burden, isn't it, being a god to your child?

We were discussing the relationship of the generations with one of my sons not long ago, and I asked: "What would you say is the outstanding attitude of the teenagers today?" His answer was short and universal: "CYNICISM about everything!" "What did his generation think of ours?" Again the answer was blunt and inclusive: "They think you're a bunch of hypocrites." Try those questions on YOUR youth, and see if the answers -- if the children are being truthful and saying what they feel and not what they think you want to hear -- see if those answers aren't frighteningly close to that.

Well, fellow paents, how do you like it? And how did it get that way?

You know, nature has equipped most animals with a

fear of things that are harmful to them. Their survival depends upon recognizing certain kinds of danger in time to avoid it. But a frog, in at least one respect, was sort of shortchanged by good old Mother Nature, because he has a certain flaw in this early warning system, which sometimes can prove fatal. If a frog, for instance, is placed in a pan of warm water and the heat is gradually increased and increased, he will typically show no inclination to escape. Since he is cold-blooded, his body temperature remains approximately the same as the water around him. He could easily hop to safety, but there he sits, thinking about something else, peering over the edge of the pan, while the clouds of steam curl ominously about him and finally he boils to death, having succumbed to a tragedy that could have easily been avoided.

How much we are like our little green friends! Oh, we react quite responsively, quickly and excitedly to sudden dangers which confront us -- war, disease epidemics, earthquakes, tornadoes -- and we are all brought into immediate mobilization and action. But if a threatening problem arises slowly, say over the period of a decade or two, we often allow ourselves to boil to death in happy ignorance.

And so we have passively accepted a slowly deteriorating "youth scene" without a croak in protest. What do you think our great grandparents would say, if they could see the juvenile problems which are being allowed to spread over our nation today? They would probably ask us if we were BLIND, DEAF AND DUMB!

Drug abuse, for instance, and addiction, is an indescribable shame among American juveniles. In 1960, for instance, there were 1,500 arrests for juvenile narcotic misuse in the State of California. In 1968, there were 30,000 -- a gain of 2,000% in just eight years!

"Time" magazine quotes Dr. Barry Ramer, the Director of the Study of Special Problems in San Francisco, as saying: "At the California Synanon

Self-Help Centers for heroin addicts, the population has gone from zero to four hundred in five years." This is where people voluntarily turn themselves in for treatment. "Heroin," he says, "is now the most available drug on the street and the most dangerous. In my wildest nightmares, I never dreamed of seeing what we are seeing today." So says Dr. Ramer.

And you and I sit here in this good, God-fearing, fine, Middle West City of Des Moines, and you know and I know that every junior high and some of the elementary schools in this city are FILLED WITH DRUGS! And we don't have the guts to demand that someday, without warning, they strip down those schools, locker by locker, student by student, and find out what's really there. We haven't got the GUTS to do it, because we're afraid of what we'd find!

Young people are now playing another dangerous game, neatly packaged under the title of "sexual freedom." The rationale sounds very plausible: "Why should we be restricted by the hang-ups and prohibitions and restrictions of past generations? Why not ENJOY one of the greatest of life's pleasures as much and as often and with as many as you can? Now that God is dead, who has the authority to deny us this fulfillment?" No, illicit sex is not a new problem. That's been going on for thousands of years, with this difference: IMMORALITY HAS NEVER BEFORE BEEN RIGHT OR PROPER, as it is in America today. "Bed today -- marry tomorrow -- maybe," that's the motto.

You know, I lived for four years in a fraternity house at the university -- four years with about forty real men -- and I never saw a young lady on the second floor living quarters or bedrooms of that fraternity in those four years. So I am still a little unaccustomed to visiting my son at the University of Iowa and having a young lady walk into his room unannounced and uninvited. But, you see, we have to give them this FREEDOM! They DEMAND it!

A young psychologist, Dr. James Dobson, says this: "Without being unnecessarily pessimistic, it is accurate to say that the traditional Christian concept of morality is DEAD among the majority of high school students in America today. Teachers tell me of their surprise at the blatant ADMISSIONS of immorality made by their students." I often talk to high school groups on this subject. It's the first time in my life that I have ever had a group of kids ARGUE with me about the position I took or tell me in so many words that I didn't know what I was talking about.

Another of our symptoms of adolescent unrest is seen in the frequent display of aggression and hostility. According to F.B.I. figures, arrests for juvenile assault have increased 70% faster than the rest of the population in the last two years. Right now, two-thirds of the crimes of violence (assault, murder and rape) are committed by juveniles. Along with these are the emotional maladjustments, the gang warfare, the teenage suicide, the school failures, and the students' attacks on their teachers. One teacher, an athlete, six feet, five inches tall, 220 pounds, quit his job because he was AFRAID of his students. Not long ago, one student approached his high school teacher in the parking lot of the school, poked a shotgun into his belly and demanded the keys to his car and his money. The teacher brushed the gun away, laughed, and walked on. And the psychiatrist says: "He didn't realize what an awful chance he was taking, because with the drugs floating around, he had no assurance that that child would not have fired that gun." One girl home from her freshman semester at the University of Iowa has asked to talk to me about two girlfriends who are threatening suicide. And Senator John McClellan points out that in all of this a criminal -- be he juvenile or adult -- has a one in twenty chance of being apprehended for his crime or brought to trial for it. A one in twenty chance! That's pretty good odds, isn't it? Let me be clear. ALL OF THIS IS NOT TO

CONDEMN OUR YOUTH! It is to point us up as the frogs we are who are BOILING TO DEATH, and we don't even know it! How did they get this way? There is only one obvious answer. Children's attitudes are not born in them. They didn't come with their genes. Children's attitudes, values and morality are TAUGHT. Who taught them? Well, who were their priests? Parents? Teachers? Advisors? You name it. What were they taught? Their priests believed, in the last decade, that successful parenthood consists in two primary obligations: first, to raise a child in an atmosphere of genuine affection; and secondly, to satisfy his every material and physical need. That takes care of parenthood.

At a recent convention of child psychologists in Los Angeles, the keynote speaker made the statement that THE GREATEST SOCIAL DISASTER IN THIS CENTURY WAS THE BELIEF THAT ABUNDANT LOVE MAKES DISCIPLINE UNNECESSARY. So, during the last two decades, our children have been sacrificed on the altar of overindulgence, permissiveness and smother love. All of the coveted goodies of our affluent society have been heaped upon them; and, in return, instead of getting the gratitude, the appreciation and the love that we hope to elicit, we receive, as parents, only antagonism and haughty contempt! Why? Because we have never understood that love and discipline are not antithetical. LOVE AND DISCIPLINE ARE NOT ANTITHETICAL! One is the function of the other.

As one young girl, in very grave trouble, said to me: "My parents, Pastor, gave me EVERYTHING, except a good beating when I needed one." A parent must convince himself that punishment is not something he does TO a child. It's something he does FOR a child. His attitude, whether it's toward his own child or any other child, must be "I love you too much to allow you to do that." That will impress them with your love. We're afraid of our chilren.

A few days ago, a father and mother called me about their fourteen-year-old girl. She was defying them by keeping constant late and early company with a high school dropout bum who was part of a drinking, pot smoking, sex exploitation gang. The parents REQUESTED the girl if she please would not see this young man anymore, and she used the oldest, childhood blackmail in the game and said: "If you forbid me to see him, I'll run away from home." You know, we're not afraid of what our children will do to us, it's what they'll do to our vaunted community image that is so precious to us. We don't care about THEM. It's just our image that concerns us. You know, there's a very simple answer to that "running away" question. It was used by all three of our children. The answer is: "Well, all right, I DO forbid you. Now, let's go and I'll help you pack." And you know, none of them ever left. Suckers! Strangely, children do not leave home because of wise, rigid, and loving discipline. They leave home for LACK of it. Any child psychologist or worker with runaway children will tell you that.

What about morals? Dr. J. D. Unwin, a British social anthropologist, spent seven long years studying the birth and death of eighty civilizations. He reported from these exhaustive, documented studies that every known civilization had followed the same sexual patterns. During its early days, premarital and extramarital relationships were strictly forbidden. The people had great social and industrial energy, and the culture prospered. But much later in its history, the people began to rebel against these strict prohibitions, demanding freedom and release from their internal passions and needs. And as the morals weakened, the social energy abated, eventually resulting in the decay and destruction of each of these civilizations. And so Dr. Unwin concludes: "Any human society is free either to display great energy, or to enjoy sexual freedom. The evidence is absolutely overwhelming that they cannot do both for more than a generation." Now, do you tell me that the United States of America is going to be different than the whole story of history?

Washington, in his Farewell Address to the nation, told us: "The foundation of this republic is morality. Without morality, it cannot exist." America is through. But he further said: "It is stupid to believe that we can have morality without a religious motivation." So we go on telling our little, Godless kids: "Be good, now. Be good! Be good!" And finally they say: "Why?" What do you say then? "Well, virtue is its own reward." Virtue is for suckers! "Crime doesn't pay!" Not from where I'm sitting. It pays pretty good. One resigned President is going to make a couple of million dollars at least on a book. Crime pays!

Dr. Dobson said that when his daughter is ten years old, he is going to give her a little golden key on a chain to wear around her neck, and he's going to tell her that it is the key to herself. It is the symbol of her virginity, and she can only use it once, and she has to give it to the person who uses it. And he hopes that it will be the man she loves and marries for the rest of her life. I wish that every little girl of ten were given such a key and told what it meant and explained what it meant to lose it, or use it, that it can only be used once, and then you have unlocked yourself to all.

The most important part of our priesthood as a parent is to show in ourselves that the child's Heavenly Father is like we are -- a loving, but DISCIPLINING parent. The Bible's theme from Genesis to Revelation about parenthood is summed up in the Book of Proverbs, as it says: "He that spareth the rod, hateth his son." Do you want it any clearer than that? HE THAT SPARETH THE ROD, HATETH HIS SON! Or as it says in the New Testament in the Book of Hebrews: "Bring your child up in Christian discipline as a good disciple of Christ."

You know, in a large church family, it's difficult to

know everyone personally, but you may be sure of this, that each year, I become very well acquainted with about one hundred people. They are the parents, the fathers and mothers, of my confirmands. You would be surprised how well I know their parents, after they've gone through a year of confirmation. I have, indeed, only to look at the attendance record and see that the child is there on Wednesdays at the class, but on Sunday, when the child was supposed to be in Church School or Worship with his parents, he was absent. I wish you could read the notes that I get. Some are legitimate, but others make me want to regurgitate.

May God forgive the parents, many of them, who have demitted their priesthood. How will they explain to God the destruction of a LIFE that was not theirs but that was loaned to them? As Christ said: "Better for them that a millstone be hung around their neck and they be put in the deepest part of the ocean." DO YOU THINK JESUS CHRIST WAS KIDDING?

The basis of all morality and Christian fidelity is discipline, and children cannot learn discipline from UNdisciplined slobs of parents. When God said to all of us: "Honor thy father and thy mother," it was TAKEN FOR GRANTED that the father and mother were WORTHY of honor.

Well, how's our priesthood going?

Handling the Future

*"We are afflicted in every way, but not crushed;
perplexed, but not driven to despair; persecuted, but not
forsaken; struck down, but not destroyed; always
carrying in the body the death of Jesus, so that the life of
Jesus may also be manifested in our bodies. For while we
live we are always being given up to death for Jesus'
sake, so that the life of Jesus may be manifested in our
mortal flesh."*

(II Corinthians 4:8-11 RSV)

*****

In dealing with the future, we have, apparently,
succumbed to two heresies. They seen antithetical, yet
both heresies. The one is pessimism. Things are in a
terrible mess. The man said: "Cheer up, things could be
worse," and he was right, they were worse. Things are
bad, and they are going to stay bad. The world is what it
is because of the rottenness of human nature, and you
can't change human nature. You will notice that
pessimism is always mixed up with a kind of pagan

fatalism. What will be, will be. We are all playthings in the hands of an angry God, and after He is through playing games with us, He swats us like flies, and it's curtains.

Like the conversation I heard between two cab drivers the other morning, "Did you hear about Joe?" "Yeah, too bad." "How old was he?" "Only 52." "Well, that's the way it is. When ya gotta go, ya gotta go." Things are the way they are. You can't change anything, so why struggle? Hope is just a silly illusion. Nothing is going to get better. How can the future bring happiness to me?

Like the woman whose psychiatrist insisted that she take a vacation to help cure her depression. After a few days, she wrote to him: "I'm having a wonderful time. I wish you were here to tell me why." I sat next to a man on a plane not long ago who was able to sum up the hopelessness of our situation in three brief sentences: "There are too many Communists and Socialists in the government. There are too many Jews in the business world. And there are too many Niggers everywhere." He had solved all of life's problems the easy way. There was nothing to be done! Here is a kind of twisted, neurotic hatred toward life, toward the world and everything in it. Hopelessness becomes an excuse for all of life's failures and frustrations.

Surely the disease has afflicted the youth of our day. One college student put it to me bitterly: "There is one big difference between your generation and ours. You expect to live out your lives and die of natural causes. We don't." A generation ago, our elders had to confront us with the hard facts of life to take a little of the optimism out of us, to sober us up, not allowing our hopes for the future to become too high. Well, you don't have to do that with youth today. They don't have any hope. It's smart to be cynical, jaded, disillusioned. Life at the bottom is meaningless and futile, and so as I heard one young man put it: "You live it up, and to hell with it!"

Religion is hopeful, and so religion is just more childish stupidity, illusory nonsense.

A modern poet represents one of these irreligious young women who reaches the last desperate straits of hopelessness:

"Luminal is what you take
For heartbreak
That is all,
Except sometimes allonal or
Veronal.

Prayer was useful, so they say,
In a sentimental day,
You arose from kneeling, sure
God and you'd both somehow endure --
But such gestures are for us
One must say, ridiculous --
Out of date
For us young sophisticates.

Now we have our drugstore god,
With glass tubelets for his rod . . .
Three along your business day,
On the hour girls used to pray;
Luminal; allonal; veronal;
That is all."

That's it then. Life is going to play its dirty tricks, and so you just take some more nerve medicine and go on.

Suicides are increasing alarmingly in our nation, and the most alarming fact is that the greatest increase is among teenagers. So, we have become a culture of pessimists -- we are surrounded by them -- people who are never happy unless they feel miserable, people who not only expect the worst, but they make the worst of it when it happens. When they have the choice between two evils, they take both. They feel bad when they feel good, because they are afraid they'll feel worse if they feel better. These are the "Evangelists of Doom" as Dr.

Luccock calls them. They believe that optimism is a kind of neurosis and that despair is the only reality. Havelock Ellis in his book, "The Dance of Life," insists that the only place that optimism flourishes is in an insane asylum.

Descriptive of it is Samuel Beckett's play, "Waiting for Godot." There is no play. It has no plot. Two men sit by a dead tree in the middle of the stage, and they wait. They are waiting for Godot -- God, of course. They are waiting for someone to come and redeem them, and so they talk while they are waiting. But nothing happens. No one comes. And the play ends with them still sitting there alone, beside the dead tree. This is pessimism!

Well, there's another heresy, optimism. Optimism is the kind of false hope that deceives us with protection. It's like a pacifier, as one man puts it, "that Mother Nature puts into the hands of man, her fretful child, while he is cutting his teeth on the hard realities of life." False hope that keeps the gambler throwing his money away, while he waits for that winning streak, that big killing that certainly must come. False hope that keeps the criminal going further and further into the coils of crime, always with the ever-growing illusion that he will never be caught. False hope that rationalizes all of the failures of the lazy, while they sit and wait for good fortune to smile on them, their ship to come in and drop happiness and plenty in their laps. The silly, false hope that keeps the spinster looking under the bed every night to see if there's a man hidden there. Our contemporary world is full of the tragedy of false hope.

The newsman, Charles Wells, writes of the present racial tensions: "The preachments of the Great Society touched off great expectations among the Negroes. Money poured into the slums for a few, brief months during 1965 and '66, spurring false hopes -- Head Start, the Teachers Corps, the Job Corps, Job Training. Then the dollars dried up. But HOPE did not dry up. It festered into a kind of special virus that threatens us all.

Black power entered the vaccum left by broken promises and unfulfilled hopes." This is optimism?

Remember the peace negotiations with the North Vietnamese? We were assured that the government of Hanoi was sitting at the peace table because they were hurting badly. They were defeated. They wanted out. What sheer nonsense! Fighting while negotiating, if we would only remember, is an old Communist tactic.

"Between the Lines" reported at that time that the press in Japan, Hong Kong, India and France indicated that the Viet Cong committed less than half their troops in the Tet Offensive, and yet they devastated and overran thirty of the largest cities in South Vietnam, and they had very little help from North Vietnamese troops. And that's why some observers would not take seriously the Pentagon's legend of optimism that the TET Offensive was the "last lunge," as they put it, "of a defeated enemy." I wonder where that defeated enemy got the power to assault our very headquarters in Saigon and where they are still getting the power to continue the war.

Another editor writes: "We don't share the optimism of the so-called tough police chiefs in Miami, Philadelphia and elsewhere, who bragged that there were no riots in those cities after Dr. Martin Luther King's assassination, because the Negro gangs knew our cops would shoot to kill." "With guns in the hands of thousands of Negroes in every major city, does the sheer fact of guns in the hands of tough cops assure PEACE in the future? The history of rebellion and violence doesn't support this kind of optimism," so writes another journalist. This is optimism!

The fact is that you will find no support for EITHER heresy in the Word of God -- for neither pessimism nor optimism. Christianity is not faith of Pollyanna optimism. I get so sick of hearing character improvement talks that tell us we should always be optimistic, looking on the positive side. This is not Christianity! It was born into a world without hope, very much like ours. In the Greco-Roman world of that day, hope was regarded as an evil illusion, raising men's spirits only to dash them to the ground again. But hope existed in one group -- the group which apparently had the least reason for it -- the Christians.

But there is a difference between optimism and hope. You've heard the old cliche, the illustration about the glass partly filled with water, that the pessimist looks at it and says: "Oh, the glass is half empty," and the optimist says: "The glass is half full." CHRISTIAN HOPE SAYS NEITHER! Christian hope says: "Sometimes the glass is nearly full, and then through the stupidity or sin of man, it is spilled or stolen, and it becomes almost empty; but during my lifetime, my task is to help fill the glass, and in God's good time, my cup will overflow."

For all of its brutal candor and grim realism, the Bible is a book of HOPE! It is the glowing characteristic of our Christian life and faith. It doesn't mean that we are immune to a sense of failure or frustration in life. Indeed not! We are much more sensitive to it than most people. Each of us has a secret, which, if we only realized it, we share with almost everyone else, and that is the sense of frustration and incompleteness of not doing a good job with life, not doing the kind of job that we would like to do or that we have the possibility of doing. This ailment is universal. The more we accomplish, the more we are aware of our failures. The wiser we become, the more appalled we are at our own ignorance. The more devout we are, the more conscious we are of our own sin and our guilt. The older we become, the more we are aware that the path behind us is full of wasted efforts, wrong turns, missed opportunities, broken dreams, bad decisions. Paul cries out: "It's not what I have attained, that is nothing. What I would have done, I didn't do!"

Cecil Rhodes on his deathbed mutters with his last breath: "So little done, and so much yet to do." Another famous man, dying, says: "I have scarcely started, and time says that now I must go." Why should it be, this sense of frustration, of incompleteness? What is it that life is made this way? Browning asks: "Why is it that a man's reach should exceed his grasp?" Why are we afflicted with what one theologian has called this "divine discontent?"

Ah, beloved, it is this quest itself that lures us on. At the moment a man feels that he has "arrived" -- IN THAT MOMENT, HE DIES! Life is accomplishment. Life is growth. And if we think that life is tragic because it is incomplete, there is much greater tragedy. Life can seem complete. "No," says our Lord, "the Father works yet, and I work." He tells us: "He who has begun a great work in you will bring it to perfection." That, beloved, is Christian HOPE, the sure knowledge that what we are and what we are doing has meaning. We may leave this world with all of our dreams unattained, but in God's good time and His eternity, we will see it brought to perfection, and we will have had a part in it. If there is no truth in that, then let's be honest enough to huddle together somewhere in a room and turn on the gas and have the whole farce over with.

If anything can save our lives from being sheer hypocrisy, it is Christian hope. We will hope, as a Christian, in that which God showed us on the cross that He could take the WORST SIN of man, our most IGNORANT STUPIDITIES, our most CRUEL HATREDS, our most VILE PREJUDICES, He could take all of the DESTRUCTION, the BLOODSHED, the HORROR, the HELL that we make of His world, and out of it, He can fashion His Kingdom. That is Christian hope! That is the sureness with which we face the future.

What are Browning's words? "Ah, but a man's reach SHOULD exceed his grasp, else what's heaven for?" We are not wide-eyed optimists about this world. Things are NOT getting better and better! I don't care what the Optimist Club says. Nor are we pessimists. It is not fate that makes history. It's people, people like you and me, and what we believe about the eternal values in this world. If we begin to wonder whether there is hope for saving anything from this ravaged world, then we need to remember the conviction of Albert Schweitzer:

"No lie lasts forever -- but TRUTH does.
No tyranny lasts forever -- but JUSTICE does.
No ugliness lasts forever -- but BEAUTY does.
No sin lasts forever -- but UNRIGHTEOUSNESS does."

Or, as Washington Gladden expresses Christian hope:

"I know that right is right;
That it is not good to lie;
That love is better than spite,
And a neighbor than a spy;

In the darkest night of the year,
When the stars are all gone out,
That courage is better than fear,
And faith is truer than doubt.

And fierce though the fiends may fight,
And long though the angels hide,
I know that Truth and Right
Have the universe on their side.

And that somewhere, beyond the stars,
There is a Love that is better than fate,
When the night unlocks her bars
I shall see Him, and I will wait."

"For while we live we are always being given up to death for Jesus' sake, so that the life of Jesus may be manifested in our mortal flesh."

The Seen and Unseen

"Meanwhile our eyes are fixed not on the things that are seen but on the things that are unseen; for what is seen passes away; what is unseen is eternal."
(II Corinthians 4:18 NEB)

*****

In our day, it would well seem that Paul's distinction ought to be reversed, that we are more anxiety-ridden about those things that are unseen than we are about those things that are seen. The truth is that our anxieties can work either way. That is what makes them so difficult to battle. There is enough visible evidence in the world to stimulate our fears, and the forecasts for the future are equally frightening. So our faith must serve as an antidote in both directions.

A ministerial colleague of mine tells of how his five-year-old son prayed one evening when he was ready for bed and when his father had left on a trip. "Dear God," said the boy, "help Daddy on his trip. There he is driving up that hill, and he's just had a flat tire, and he's out changing the tire, and there's a big old snake crawling up closer and closer to him, and it's just about to bite Daddy. Oh, God, don't let that happen!" As the wife told the pastor about it later, the boy had worked himself up into a shivering fear over something that had not happened and would not happen. Here was a little lad who was having his first experience at the most common disease of mankind -- anxiety. A writer in "Time" magazine gives us a revealing definition for anxiety. He says: "Anxiety is a fear in search of a cause." Quite revealing. Quite penetrating.

We don't need the poet Auden to tell us that ours is "The Age of Anxiety." Look around you. Do you see anyone who is completely unafraid? What about you? Are you afraid? Of course you are. And so is everyone else. The fact of fear is one of the facts of life -- for everyone -- for fear is no respecter of persons or ages or positions or places. No one is immune to it. A famous physician says: "The commonest and subtlest of all human diseases is fear." Fear of the future. Fear of danger. Fear of Communism. Fear of atom and hydrogen bombs. Fear of loss -- loss of health, loss of possessions, loss of position, loss of job, losses of self-esteem. Fear of failure. Fear of ridicule. Fear of exposure. Fear of being disliked. Fear of death. Fear of the unknown. "Where man can find no answer," says Norman Cousins, "he will find fear." There is a fear for every frustration, every failure, every danger in life.

An attractive young woman sits fidgeting on the edge of a chair. She has all the characteristics of a terrified bird about to take flight. Her body, her head, her eyes, flit here, there, everywhere, completely involuntarily mobile. "What are you afraid of?" I ask. "I don't know," she answers. "I guess I'm really afraid that I'm going to die." "And how does that affect you?" "I have these spells, I call them. I can be shopping, driving a car, washing the dishes -- anything -- and suddenly, without any warning, I'm terrified. I want to run. I want to flee.

But I can't move. I start to shake. I feel the heart thumping in my chest. I can't get my breath. I begin to get numb all over, and I feel like I'm going to faint, and all the while, I get more and more and more frightened." Then she paused for a moment and added: "You think I'm going crazy, don't you?" No, my dear young woman, I don't think that you are going crazy. I think that you are sick -- sick with the disease of anxiety.

Soren Kierkegaard, the great Danish philosopher, argued that most of us stop short of real personhood; that is, we don't discover our real individuality -- our spiritual natures -- because of our response to anxiety that is at the core of our personal lives. We are unnerved by crippling disturbances that refuse to let us know lasting peace of any kind. Jesus was being realistic when He said: "In the world you will have anxiety." It is a part of our common life.

I ask a college professor the same question: "What are you afraid of?" And this distinguished gentleman answers truthfully: "I don't know what it is, but there's something there. I don't even know why it should be there. All I know is that it is."

Look, will you, at that wealthy man. Money in his pockets, money in the banks, money in stocks and real estate -- but he has fear, stark fear in his heart. And what's he afraid of? Insanity. His money, his mansion, his security all mean nothing to him because he is afraid of losing his mind. Life has become a nightmare; decisions are almost impossible; his fear feeds on every hesitation, every missed appointment, every mistake that he makes. He's in sheer agony.

Look again and see that woman -- mother of three lovely children, wife of a successful and attentive husband who has provided for her a lovely home and financial security. But it all means nothing to her. Why? Because she is afraid -- afraid of cancer. Her closest friend died of it, and, ever since, there has been this fear, this black foreboding fear, gnawing in her mind and in her guts. Oh, yes, she has gone to doctors, many of them, but that doesn't satisfy her. They might have missed something. And so, her days and her nights are filled with anxiety.

Look, will you, at the "Big Man on the Campus." He's loud, he's big, he's a hail-fellow-well-met. But he's afraid. He's afraid, deep down, that all his life he's been nothing but a big bluff, a big blow, and that he really doesn't have what it takes. He tries to cover it up with loud talk and expansive gestures, but he'll face up to his fear some day -- he'll have to -- and it may be a shattering experience.

Look at -- oh, but why go on picking faces out of the crowd? You see them everywhere -- fear-ridden, fear-riddled, fear-hindered people with faces and souls etched by the acids of anxiety and fear. You might even see one when you look into the mirror. Do you?

"Fear and anxiety," says Dr. Karen Horney, the psychologist, "are both proportionate reactions to danger, but in the case of fear, the danger is a transparent, objective one, and in the case of anxiety, it is hidden and subjective."

Overstreet, the great psychiatrist, speaks of the peculiar grip of fear. "Of all the emotional forces that pattern our individual and interpersonal behavior, fear has the most insidious power," he says, "to make us do what we ought not to do, and leave undone what we ought to do. Under its influence, and trying to escape its influence, we seem fated to give it yet a stronger hold on us." Even as we fight fear, it gets more of a grip on us.

So, that's our problem. What do we do about it?

One thing is sure: it is disastrous to park by it. As Norman Vincent Peal warns: "Don't settle down and live permanently with your fears. If you do, you will never be happy. You will never be an effective human being."

But how does one move beyond fear -- beyond these fears that distort and twist and enslave and limit life? By changing locations? By going to Florida or Phoenix or Hollywood or Hawaii? No. There are anxiety-ridden people in all of those places. They tried to run away from their fears, but found their fears waiting for them when they arrived. Does one move beyond fear and anxiety by summoning one's courage and saying: "There now, be brave?" And what, pray, do you have to be brave with? No, we can't exhort ourselves out of fear and into bravery. It doesn't work, and any one of you who has gone through military combat knows that.

How, then, does one move beyond anxiety? One counselor tells about one who did.

She was a happy and efficient pastor's wife, experiencing the full share of sunshine and shade, but with no real drakness falling across her way. And then, suddenly, without warning, her husband died of a heart attack, leaving her terribly alone and terribly afraid, afraid of her own decisions, afraid of the present, afraid of the future. The counselor says: "When I saw her, she was in the vice-like grip of fear's tyranny, and so tyrannized that most of her time was spent in bed." (It is possible for a person to be so fear-ridden that he becomes bed-ridden. I know people who spend a great deal of their time in bed, simply because they are afraid.) "When I saw her two years later," the counselor said, "surprisingly, she was a poised, serene woman, working as a receptionist in an insurance office. I asked her to explain her amazing recovery." "The work helped, of course," she said, "but I couldn't work at all until I faced my fear and saw that it was basically a selfish rebellion against God and what I thought was God's will. When I saw that, I began to pray that God would forgive my selfishness, and, as I prayed, I became aware of God's hand reaching down to me, and I, somehow, began to reach up in faith, until I finally clasped that hand. And, to my amazement, I found HIS hand clasping mine, and I knew that He really cared and that He would help me as long as I held His hand in faith." Says the counselor: "As I looked at her, I saw a woman who had known for years how to talk about faith, but had only recently begun to exercise it for a deep, personal need. And I saw a stronger, more poised woman, with that certain and unmistakable maturity of the heart known only to those who, through faith, are moving beyond the crippling, shattering limitations of fear." Well, moving from fear to faith through prayer works for others, also.

Think of it -- fear of self, fear of self's inadequacies -- and oh, how many of us are afraid, are anxious about our own inadequacies -- fear of failures, all of this, plus the fear of others and other's opinions, the fear for the future. Is it any wonder that so many people are living so far below their best and most productive selves?

Notice the steps that the pastor's wife took as she moved from fear to faith: First, she had to face her fear squarely for what it was; second, she had to replace fear with faith through prayer; and third, she had to learn to live in loving honesty with herself, with God and with others. What a prescription for counteracting fear! What penicillin for despair! What therapy for the threatened!

Face your fears. Look at them. Examine them. See them for what they are. It is very often the case that your fear is just the product of an overactive imagination, that you are working yourself up into a state of agitation over something that has not happened and never will happen, like the boy and the snake and his father. We talk ourselves INTO our anxieties through our imagination. Look at your fear. See whether it's really real. In ninety-nine out of a hundred cases, it isn't.

And then, replace that fear with faith. It's never enough just to say: "Fear, be gone!" Fear must be replaced! Says Dr. William S. Sadler, the famous Jewish psychiatrist: "The only known cure for fear and anxiety is faith." That's a simple, unqualified statement. "The only known cure for fear is faith!" And that from a scientist! The road that leads from fear to faith, as the pastor's wife learned, is PRAYER. "I sought the Lord," said David, "and He heard me, and He delivered me from all my fears."

At the time of the Dunkirk disaster and retreat back in 1940 -- many of you remember that vividly -- thousands of Englishmen were gripped by a terrible fear because of the threatened German invasion of the British Isles. It was during this time that someone wrote this inscription over the entrance of the Hind's Head Hotel near Dover, that closest point to the continent. The inscription read: "Fear knocked. Faith answered: 'No one is here.' "

What do you do when fear knocks? Stand there shaking? Crumble into a quivering mass of anxiety? Lose your poise and get loud and blustery? Come out fighting wildly and blindly, expending all of your energy on phantoms? You don't have to do that. You can say with the psalmist: "What time I was afraid, I will trust in Thee." Or, better than that, say with Isaiah: "I will trust and not be afraid." That is faith: trust, trust in a loving and providential God; trust in spite of consequences.

And now to live! And so to the third step: to live in loving honesty with ourselves, with others and with God. That is more than just a step, it's a pattern for living. Strange, isn't it, how the basic principles of effective, fear-free living are the same from day to day, from person to person, from age to age. Seven hundred years before Christ, the prophet Micah asks: "What does the Lord require of thee but to do justice, to love mercy and to walk humbly with thy God." What is that but a life lived in loving honesty with ourselves, with others and with God?

Fifty years after Christ, John wrote: "There is no fear in love. Perfect love casts out fear." Paul wrote thirty years after Christ (and if any man knew the dangers, the strange turnings, the fear-producing situations, it was certainly he who did). Hear him: "God hath not given us the spirit of fear, but of power, and of love, and of a sound mind."

Listen today to the psychoanalysts and psychologists and psychiatrists:

Dr. Overstreet again: "That love is man's basic need

has become the axiom of modern therapy."

Drs. Karl and Jeanette Menninger, in their book, "Love Against Hate," state that the central problem of the psychiatrist is how to encourage love and trust and reduce fear and hate.

And Dr. Smiley Blanton, the psychiatrist, entitles his best-selling book, "Love or Perish."

There it is, then, the prescription for getting rid of the curse of anxiety:

FACE YOUR FEARS. Look at them.

REPLACE YOUR FEAR WITH FAITH THROUGH PRAYER. That's not just the pious mouthing of a preacher. That's the actuality of life. I know. It works.

And then, LIVE IN LOVING TRUST WITH YOURSELF, WITH OTHERS, AND WITH GOD.

And when fear comes knocking at YOUR door, you may be able to answer: "Sorry, there is no one here."

He Knows Not How

"And he said, 'The kingdom of God is as if a man should scatter seed upon the ground, and should sleep and rise night and day, and the seed should sprout and grow, he knows not how."

(Mark 4:26-27 RSV)

*****

Would it shock you if I confessed to you that I do not find the subject of my sermon, nor do I always have the sermon suggested to me, while reading the Bible? For example, the subject of this discussion was suggested by two things, unalike and both unbiblical.

First, a few days ago, a young woman in our parish was going through a serious crisis in her life. It was extremely difficult, I knew, for her to do what she had to do, and I assured her that God would help her through her time of trial and testing. And instantly, she retorted, almost in a sneer: "Look, Pastor, you know I've always been a good church member, but the first time I really NEED God, He's nowhere around. I've prayed and I got no answer. I asked for help, and then I knew that what I'm going to do, I'm going to have to do by myself. In all of this, I don't even know whether God exists or not. I've searched, but I can't find Him." To which I answered, not "join the group," but "join the multitude," not of people who have had this experience but of people who THINK they have had this experience and say that they have had this experience.

Secondly, the other day I picked up my wife's copy of the "Ladies' Home Journal," because I noticed an article by a secular author named Malcolm Muggeridge entitled, "Is There a God?" Sick to death of people telling me of how they searched for God and prayed to God and sought His help -- all of which is a lot of polite and pious hogwash -- I was immediately attracted to the article by the first paragraph. Here was a writer who, at long last, began at least where every such article should begin and where every human being, if he is honest and candid, MUST begin. The words were certainly a welcome relief. "Is there a God?" May I quote the first lines:

"Well, is there? I myself should be very happy to answer with an emphatic negative. Tempermentally, it would suit me very well to settle for what the world offers, and to write off as wishful thinking, or just the self-importance of the human species, any notion of divine purpose and a divinity to entertain and execute it. The earth's sounds and smells and colors are very sweet; human love brings golden hours; the mind at work earns delight. I have never wanted a God, or feared a God, or felt under any necessity to invent one."

You want to make it Biblical, so that you can go home and say that you heard a sermon based on the Bible? The Old Testament: Job -- immersed in his woes, deeper and deeper in the slough of despair, his friends saying, "But you are a godly man. Call upon God and surely He will answer you and help you." That was sheer, cynical sarcasm. They didn't believe that God would or could. Job didn't either. He cried out: "Oh, if I knew where I might find Him. I go forward, and He is not there; backward and I perceive Him not. I turn to the left and to the right, and I cannot see Him."

But the ancient psalmists had beat him to it. One wept: "My tears have been my meat night and day, while continually they say unto me, 'Where is your God?'" Another psalmist: "As with a sword in my bones my enemies reproach me and say unto me daily, 'Where is your God?'" You want the New Testament? What could be more authentic than the words of Christ from the cross: "My God, my God, why hast thou forsaken ME?" The people about the cross? "He called upon God. Let's see if anyone answers." They didn't believe anyone would.

All right. Things are going well for you? You can sing lustily "Praise God from whom all blessings flow." Seems only the decent thing to do, doesn't it? But what about the other times? How well do you sing the words of the old hymn, "Nearer, My God, to Thee?"

"Though like a wanderer,
The sun gone down,
Darkness be over me,
My rest a stone,
So by my woes to be
Nearer, my God, to thee."

Really, how many of us can sing that? "So by my WOES to be nearer, my God, to thee." Not many, I venture. We're all tempted to sit in the seat of Job and cry: "Oh, that I might find Him. I look, but when I need Him, He's not there." And yet, if we are going to find God, that's where we must. We don't live too many years on this old globe before we discover what Keats has called "the giant agony of the world." More and more the dreadful contradiction appears between our Christian faith and the hideous, tragic evil on this earth. We become like the little boy who was asked by his teacher to tell the shape of the world, and he replied: "My father says it's in the worst shape it's ever been in."

So, let us not mince matters. There's a dark side of this universe which, at least at first sight, seems utterly inconsistent with faith in a good God. Consider what we read in the newspapers. A volcano erupts, killing people, burning villages, destroying farm lands. An earthquake destroys a whole city, slaying thousands. Lightning blasts an aircraft, which falls in a blazing mass upon a house, killing the entire family, as well as the passengers. Rivers overflow their banks in disastrous floods, demolishing churches and homes and schools, exhibiting a ruthless kind of indifference toward everything that the Christian faith holds sacred. Such pitiless events are NOT human sin; they are nature's deeds. As John Stuart Mill put it: "In sober truth nearly all the things which men are hanged or imprisoned for doing to one another are Nature's everyday performances."

Why the ruthless, evolutionary process -- parasites, insects, beasts with claws and beaks. preying on each other? Why the cancer cell and the plague? Why little children born blind, deformed, perhaps as Mongolian idiots? And when one turns from nature's pitiless acts to man's, the suffering is so dreadful that one wonders how any God -- if there be one -- can stand it. So, in one of Richard Jeffries' books, a young boy looks at the picture of Christ's crucifixion, and he becomes so disturbed by its cruelty that he turns the page to hide it from his sight, saying: "If God had been there, He wouldn't have let them do it." And yet, paradoxically, it is at Calvary that we must find the Christian faith most fully revealed.

Well, that's where we must find Him. But do we? What is the normal response for many of us? It is skepticism, cynicism, fatalism, or perhaps a kind of hidden, secret atheism. That's not unusual. The first impulse of Job was atheism, the first words of our author, Muggeridge. It's the common experience of all of us. Martin Luther was a man of tremendous faith, but once he wrote: "Who among men can understand the full meaning of this Word of God, 'Our Father who art in

heaven?' Anyone who genuinely believes these words
will often say, 'While I am affirming this faith, then my
Father suffers me to be thrown into prison, drowned, or
beheaded,' and then faith falters, and in weakness I cry,
'Who knows whether it is true or not?' "

We are, many of us, like the American surgeon who
says that if he ever comes face to face with God, he will
hold up a cancer cell before the Almighty and demand
that He answer the question, "WHY? WHY, GOD?"

We say to ourselves that faith is just credulity,
wishful thinking. It's sugar coating the bitter pill of life
with a lush and comfortable Gospel. It is a psychological
drug, a daydream, a tranquilizer, a soothing fantasy. Dr.
Harry Emerson Fosdick is typical. He writes, autobio-
graphically: "When I was a sophomore in college, I
cleared God out of my universe and started over to see
what I could find. I dreaded being credulous, and some of
the stuff handed out to me as being part and parcel of the
Christian faith seemed to me -- and still seems to me --
incredible. But by DISbelieving in God, I did not escape
belief; I ran headlong INTO belief in atheism,
materialism, into faith that the ultimate creative factors
in the universe are physical particles operating blindly
without mind behind them or purpose in them. Talk
about credulity! I had to have it for that!"

That's the trouble, you see, friends. Just when we
think we've fastened on something more satisfying than
the traditional, childish, credulous faith, we find out that
it's false, too. We just can't live there. And so, the
Christian faith is just a soft retreat from life into a snug,
little harbor of wishful thinking? Like the words of
Whittier's hymn that we like to sing so often:

"Drop thy still dews of quietness,
'Til all our strivings cease."

Isn't that a soft retreat? Lydia Pinkham's for pious
old ladies. To which I answer: "Read Whittier's
biography. Find that he was a courageous, militant,
social reformer." In his elder years, famous as a poet, he

wrote: "I set a higher value on my name appended to the Antislavery Declaration of 1833 than on the title page of any book." I think of him at Concord, New Hampshire, on his way to address an antislavery meeting, meeting a crowd along the way who pelted him with rotten eggs until his black, Quaker coat ran yellow with the stains of them. But he stood his ground. Read all that; remember it -- and then go back to the hymn and ask where he got his stability and stamina to "fight the good fight."

Genuine Christian faith and life are NOT anything that the soft and cowardly spirit would want to retreat into. You see, you have to explain people like Whittier, if you want to make that line stick. And I get so SICK of hearing STUPID people make that accusation that "the Christian faith is a refuge for the gutless;" and yet, they don't have the brains or the courage to EXPLAIN men like Whittier and a thousand like him who have ten times the guts and courage they have!

Or you say you want some philosophy of life that faces its realities in a clear, hardheaded, unemotional way? I knew a young college student who, for instance, had decided to accept the philosophy of Schopenhauer because Schopenhauer sounded objective, rational, realistic, unemotional. He welcomed Schopenhauer's assertion that there is no God, that nothing is worth our striving, that the business of life is one that does not cover expenses, and that the only honest wish that a man can have is one for complete annihilation. "There," said the young man, "is clear, cold reason, unaffected by emotion or fancy."

Schopenhauer's atheism unaffected by emotion, my all-wise young student? When you were looking at Schopenhauer's objectivity, you were not being objective. His grandmother was insane; his father, married to an unfaithful wife, committed suicide. Then his mother turned openly to free love, for which Schopenhauer, like Hamlet, hated her vehemently; and she returned his hatred in full, until, finally, she threw him bodily, down the stairs out of their home. For the last twenty-four years of her life, Schopenhauer never saw his mother. He had no wife. He had one illegitimate son whom he would not acknowledge as his. He had no home life, few friends. He distrusted mankind so deeply that he would allow no stranger in his home. He slept always with a gun under his pillow. And Schopenhauer's atheism was OBJECTIVE? RATIONAL? SCHOLARLY? UNEMOTIONAL? POPPYCOCK! Just the stuff some stupid, uninformed student would swallow! Give him a good father and mother, a devoted wife and fine children and real friends and see how long he went on talking about the meaninglessness of life.

Do you see what I'm driving at? You are saying that folks often believe in God for emotional reasons? Because such faith is consoling and comfortable? I am saying now that many people DISBELIEVE in God for emotional reasons, because in their misery and their despair, their hopelessness, life FEELS Godless and meaningless. And I am certainly sure that atheism is commonly NOT the conclusion of a clear, cool, analytical, unemotional, objective and rational mind. Don't ever tell me that! You can't support it! You'll NEVER support it!

Oh, you can accept that view of things. Anyone can. You can go along with Clarence Darrow and say of life: "The outstanding fact that cannot be dodged by man is the futility of it all." Or, you can go along with H. L. Mencken: "Life, fundamentally, is not worth living. What could be more logical than suicide, and what could be more preposterous than keeping alive?" These are able, and thoughtful, and intelligent men. They take the way that Job's wife suggested he take: "Curse God and die." That's one alternative, if you like.

What are we saying, essentially? That you may cross God out of your life completely, or you may find Him a living reality, but the point where you DO one or the other is not going to be in some thoughtful moment of quiet and scholarly contemplation, nor is it going to be on some sunshiny day when life is serene and comfortable. We lose God completely or we find Him vitally in the darkest hours of human despair, when we face the contradictions of an evil world, when it well seems that the face of God -- if one exists at all -- is completely hidden from us. And in the moment, you can, of course, rule God out -- but then be prepared, my friend, to rule LIFE out!

You'll find as Dr. Erwin Edman, the head of Philosophy at Columbia, says of people who make this choice: "They find that this God whom they have read out, or presumed to be read out of the universe, has carried with Him into oblivion any discernible direction of things, any significance of life and any logic of destiny." Maybe you can go on living like that. I can't, and I don't think many THINKING people can.

Take Shelley, for example. He signed himself "Percy Shelley, atheist." But when John Keats died suddenly, Shelley was stirred to the depths. His faith in eternal beauty poured out of him in inspired verse, as though he had clean forgotten that he had termed himself an atheist. Here were his lines:

"The One remains, the many change and pass;
Heaven's light forever shines, earth's shadows
        fly;
Life, like a dome of many-coloured glass,
Stains the white radiance of Eternity,
That Light whose smile kindles the Universe,
That Beauty in which all things work and move."

What picture of God Shelley was rejecting when he called himself an atheist, I don't know, but this, obviously, is the work of a man who believed in the "One" eternal and beautiful. In the dark hour, he had found and seen the One whom he had said was not there.

Muggeridge writes in the "Ladies Home Journal" article: "If God were dead, and eternity had stopped, what a blessed relief to one and all! Then we could set about making a happy world in our own way -- happy in the woods like Mellors and Lady Chatterley; happiness successfully pursued along with life and liberty, in accordance with the Philadelphia specification; happy in the prospect of that Great Red Apocalypse, when the state has withered away and the proletariat reigns for evermore. If only God were D. H. Lawrence or Franklin D. Roosevelt, or Karl Marx! Alas, dead or alive, He is still God, and eternity ticks on even though all the clocks have stopped. I agree with Kierkegaard that 'what man naturally loves is finitude,' and that involvement through God in infinitude 'kills in him, in the most painful way, everything in which he really finds his life, shows him his own wretchedness, keeps him in sleepless unrest.' The fugitive from God has nowhere to turn. Even if, as a last resort, he falls back on stupefying his senses with alcohol or drugs or sex, the relief is but short-lived. Either he will sink without trace forever into the slough, or, emerging, have to face the inescapable confrontation, and it is a fearful thing to fall into the hands of the living God -- thus Kierkegaard, and also Cromwell, groaned in desperation."

"What living God?" says Muggeridge. "A being with whom one has a relationship. On the one hand, inconceivably more personal than the most intimate human one, to the point that, as we are told, God has actually counted the hairs on every head; on the other, so remote that in order to establish a valid relationship at all, it is necessary to die, to murder one's own flesh with the utmost ferocity and to better down one's ego as one would a venomous, deadly snake."

Or take a look at the life of the Father of our Country. In 1754, George Washington, a young man in his early twenties, was in a tough spot. He had been defeated at Fort Necessity. He was accused of taking hasty action before reinforcements arrived, in order to gain all of the glory for himself. His officers were called "drunken debauchees." His report on French plans was denounced as a crooked scheme in order to advance the interests of private land holders, like himself. It looked like the end of George Washington. But now, Douglas Freeman, his biographer, looking back, writes this: "Just when one is about to exclaim about such mistreatment, 'What an outrage!' one stops and reconsiders, and then says, 'What a preparation!' " For years later, when Washington knelt in the bloodstained snows of Valley Forge, he knew who it was before whom he knelt. He didn't know when he was a young man.

Moses -- a murderer, a fugitive from justice, spent forty years wandering, homeless, lost -- he found God. Paul -- wandering, alone, heartsick, ineffectual, in the Arabian desert -- he found God. Muggeridge says: "I didn't want a God. I didn't need a God. I had no desire to invent one, as some men accuse us of doing. I don't want God! But, unfortunately, I have been forced to face the fact that God wants me."

Well, ask it, friend, for yourself. Is there a God?

Why Are You Afraid?

"Why are you afraid? Have you no faith?"

(Mark 4:4a RSV)

*****

Why are you afraid? That's a good question, isn't it? In April, 1970, we talked about the disappointment suffered by the astronaut Tom Mattingly when he had to be replaced on the crew of Apollo 13 Lunar Mission. We didn't know then that a few hours later, that moon flight would become a demonstration to the whole world of something that I wanted to talk to you about.

The flight was progressing with uninterrupted smoothness. Everything was routine, even a little boring. The public, trained by now to take such un-eventful perfection for granted, was not paying much attention. They were scarcely aware that there was another mission headed for the moon. And then, with the speed of lightning, disaster struck. A sudden explosion ripped through the service module. Like a wounded animal bleeding, the spacecraft began to spew its life-giving and power-giving oxygen out into space. Power in the command module was cut off. In the twinkling of an eye, a routine, redundant, repetitious operation had become the most frightening situation ever faced by man in space.

Radio and television programs were interrupted, as the news of the crisis swept across the nation and, indeed, around the listening world. With the news came fear, like a dark cloud. Fear gripped the public. Fear galvanized the control team in the Houson-manned Space Center. And fear was struck to the hearts of the Apollo crew. And if you naively think that there was not fear, then you don't know anything about human emotions or human reactions. Describe the astronauts, if you will, as cool, controlled or courageous, but don't say that they were FEARLESS. You might as well say that they were BRAINLESS!

A citation for a battle decoration may describe a fighting man as "sacrificially brave above and beyond the call of duty," but a citation never reports -- I have never heard one or read one yet -- that a man was fearless. The senior officers who write those citations know better. To say that a man in military combat is FEARLESS would be, virtually, to say that he is STUPID!

Jesus was continually confronted with the problem of fear. The words "fear," "troubled," "anxious," and "afraid" were often in His speech. "Fear not. Be not overanxious." "Let not your heart be troubled, neither let it be afraid." He spoke often thus, for He often met fear in the lives of those whom He loved.

Some years ago, Basil King wrote a book entitled "The Conquest of Fear," and he prefaced the book with these words: "When I say that most of my life I have been the prey of fear, I take it that I am expressing the case of most people. I cannot remember a time when a dread of one kind or another was not in the air. In childhood, it was the fear of going to bed. Later, it was the fear of school. Later still, the experience in the morning of waking with a feeling of dismay at all the work that had to be done before the night. In one form or another, fear dogs every one of us: the mother afraid for her children; the father afraid for his business; the clerk afraid for his job; hardly a man that is not afraid that some other man will do him a bad turn; hardly a woman that is not afraid that what she craves may be denied or what she loves may be snatched away . . . I am ready to guess," says Mr. King, "that all the miseries wrought by sin and sickness put together would not equal those we bring on by the means which, perhaps, we do the least to counteract."

Well, you may or may not agree with the conclusions to which Mr. King later comes in his book, but you MUST agree with his premise -- that fear is a major problem in human life.

If we are to face the problem of fear constructively and in a Christian way, we had better begin going deeper than most of us do, deep enough to recognize the important function of fear and the constructive, positive purpose of fear in human development. Many books written on the subject are nothing more than delightful little treatises on how to get rid of fear, or how to master or conquer it. They are negative and unsatisfying because they start out with the false premise that fear is an enemy, an evil and harmful emotion to be completely driven out. You will not win, if you start from there. You never come out right from a false start; and that IS a false start.

Fear, rather, is an elemental emotion, a part of our native equipment, God-given; and, therefore, like any other normal emotion, it has a constructive, essential purpose. Our real problem is not to get rid of it, but how to use it constructively.

The animals are certainly aware of its purpose. There is no animal without fear. Fortunately, the frothy theory that fear is abnormal has not yet reached the chipmunk. He hasn't read the book. That is why he is still alive and chattering outside of my window, while the dog lies frustrated inside looking at him. For some creatures, like the deer and the rabbit, fear is the sole means of defense. It is not an enemy, but an ally. The sense of impending danger starts a nervous reaction which, quicker than you can say "rabbit," shoots a powerful stimulant from his glands into his running apparatus, and he is gone with the wind -- gone with the speed that he could never imagine or manage without the stimulus of fear. Any deer that can't leap at least ten feet out of an afternoon nap and come down with his feet pounding in a dead run will not live long in a forest of wolves.

We have the same equipment in our human bodies, but, in us, it is linked up with more than just glands or legs. It is all geared with our thinking machinery and our more complex emotional machinery. Human fear is an immensely complicated thing; that is why we must be more realistic in our understanding of its function. Those little books on getting rid of it just don't reach the problem. The fact is we are not ready to rid ourselves of fear. There are still too many potential muggers in the bushes and too many speeding cars on the highways for me to afford that luxury.

At our house, as our children were growing up, we taught them to keep alive some healthy fears. We wanted them to be afraid of some things -- of playing with matches and rusty razor blades, of playing in the busy street, of drinking unknown liquids out of bottles. Not all of our fears are groundless or wasted. Some of the worst of them are rooted in a reality that no amount of self-deception can drive out.

In "Moby Dick," the captain said: "I will have no man in my boat who is not afraid of a whale." I certainly don't want any airline pilot flying MY airplane who is not afraid of a thunderhead. Fear of some things is, indeed, the beginning of wisdom!

Furthermore, we are not ready to dispense with fear in the building of a society. We are not yet ready to scrap our Police Department or our law courts or even Congress. For a long time yet, we will have to go on making and enforcing laws that strike FEAR to the hearts of certain elements. There are still many persons who will not do right for right's sake, and they must be deterred by a healthy fear of the consequences.

People sometimes say: "If you do not draw us by love, you can never drive us by fear." Poppycock! Why do you pay your income tax? Because you LOVE to write checks to the government? Maybe. But insofar as the government is concerned, the threat of a penalty is a help. Why do you take out fire insurance? Because you like having insurance agents around all the time? Why do you lock your doors at night, just to exercise the locks? Let's face it. We are motivated by fears every day of our lives; and moved by fear, we do many good and constructive things. That is exactly what fear is for. It is the friend of the order, the buttress of morality, the ally of the Kingdom of God.

And now, having said that, we should pause for a clarifying word. Certainly, we should not ignore the considerable army of dedicated people whose passion it is to help us to control and conquer fear. We must agree with them that fear is an emotion of extremely high voltage, and that when it overshoots the mark or overleaps the proper boundaries, it becomes a destructive and disintegrating force. Phobias can be fatal!

Have you ever counted the phobias in your dictionary? Their name is legion; and they are all bad. There is acrophobia, or fear of height; claustrophobia, fear of closed places. There is agoraphobia, the fear of open places; neophobia, the fear of the new; pathophobia, the fear of disease; photophobia, the fear of light; spermaphobia, the fear of germs; ergophobia, the fear of work (that isn't in your dictionaries yet, but I think it will be in the next edition, considering the prevalence and the popularity of that one). More than seventy-five phobias are listed, all the way from ereuthophobia, the fear of blushing (and we could certainly use a little more of that one), to phobophobia, the fear of all things.

These are abnormal, irrational fears, not funny, but tragic. Monstrous evil comes out of misused fear, fear that overshoots its mark. They all illustrate and underscore what we are trying to say here -- that our basic problem is not how to get rid of fear, but how to use it as God meant it to be used -- as the beginning, as the starting point of WISDOM!

Consider, first the constructive use of fear AS A SPUR TO KNOWLEDGE. What a man fears most, perhaps, is the unknown -- the shapeless shadows of evil that lurk in the darkness of his ignorance. The torment of fear has been the beginning of wisdom in so many areas of life that we are almost tempted to say: "Thank God for the fears that stimulate thought! Thank God for the fear of disease that has caused men to work in a thousand laboratories, hunting for causes and cures. Thank God for the fear of want and hunger that has prodded man to invention and conservation; for the fear of ignorance that has sent them on the search for knowledge." That is what fear is for; it is a prod to the emotions, a torment in man's soul to drive him out of the darkness into light.

The emotion that affected most people, including the crew, when the explosion occurred on Apollo 13 was the fear of the unknown. Neither the crew nor the ground control team in Houston knew what had happened. All of these men had been trained to have a healthy fear of the unexpected, the accident, the malfunction. They knew only too well that some things could be fatal. But they also knew that packed into the memory of their computers was the procedure to be followed in every possible emergency. Their FEAR was, therefore, their PROD to identify the trouble, to eliminate the unknown. Their fear sharpened their wits, increased their speed, pinpointed their concentration.

What we might have identified as coolness under

pressure and calm in tension was actually fear -- fear functioning at its highest and most constructive pitch. Did you notice how, as soon as the problem had been identified and the proper procedures put into action, the crew and the controllers and the general public all relaxed and settled down to sweat out the rest of the flight? Knowledge had dispelled most of the fear.

As a rule, we are not afraid of a thing when we know what the thing is. Some people fear the dark. Why? Because they don't know what it is. They do not understand its sounds and shadows. Shakespeare said:

"Oft in the night, imagining some fear,
How easy is a bush supposed to be a bear."

We are not afraid in the broad daylight, for then we can see that a bush is a bush. Light makes the difference. Jesus said: "You shall know the truth, and the truth shall make you free." Exactly! A competent psychologist works on this principle. He knows that many of our irrational fears are rooted in some past experience, in some hidden dread buried deep in the darkness of our unconscious.

A man went to a psychiatrist, complaining of his inability to sleep at night. He heard voices always, speaking in the night. "What do the voices say?" the psychiatrist asked. "They say: 'Is he asleep yet?' " Well, after a great deal of digging into the memories of the past events in the man's life, he finally remembered that those were the last words that he heard the surgeon say just before he underwent an operation that he had had to have several years before: "Is he asleep yet?" So, once the fear was dragged out into the light, taken a look at, the fear was dispelled; and the man was able to sleep once more.

Move a step further, now, and consider fear AS A HEALTHY STIMULUS TO FAITH. I am well aware that we usually present it as just the opposite -- the enemy of faith, a shattering emotion that shrivels the faith and takes the heart out of people. Misused, it can do that. Let a person try to sing with the fingers of fear gripping his throat. Let him try to play the piano with trembling hands. Let him try to make a speech with shaking knees. And almost always, he will fail.

I have married couples standing before the altar, whom I am sure did not hear a word that I said. Harmless as this little lady seems to be, I have seen big, strong men so frightened, so paralyzed by fear, that they couldn't even get the ring on the dainty, bridal finger. Fear can paralyze us. Some persons never get started in their life work because of their fear that they will fail. This is what happens when fear overshoots its mark.

The truth is that we are stronger and tougher than we think we are -- every one of us. We have reserves of strength and powers that need, sometimes, only the stimulus of a crisis and fear to arouse them. Fear of defeat has often thrown a nation back to God to renew its strength, arouse its manhood. Fear, thus, is the foundation of faith. As President Nixon said, never has the nation and the whole world been so drawn together in prayer as when we prayed for the safe return of the astronauts. Fear had, for a change, prodded us into praying.

Above all, fear should be considered as a SPUR TO RIGHTEOUSNESS AND A HEALTHY STIMULUS TO LOVE. Here, again, we so often think of it in opposite terms; as the foe of goodness, as the age-old enemy of love. Misused, it is always that! "Perfect love casteth out fear," the New Testament tells us. There is no FEAR in LOVE. True! But there IS REAL FEAR in unrighteousness. There is real fear in unrighteousness and therein lies our hope. God planted fear in our moral natures to make us uneasy with our sins. He will never let us BE WRONG and FEEL RIGHT. We can't do it. We can't do the wrong thing and feel right about it. The fear is planted there.

You know what a toothache is and how quickly it will send you to a dentist. Like pain in the body, fear in the soul is a distress signal, warning of some inner wrongness, a healthy prod to do something constructive to correct the wrongness. Put wrong in your life, and you put fear into it. Are you afraid? Put WRONG in your life, and you have put FEAR into it! And then someday, somewhere, the alarm bell sounds, and that is what we are hearing now -- all over the earth -- the loud sounding of the alarm, warning us of inner wrongs and sins and evils to be set right before the world can be right.

One of the crucial problems of this hour is the problem of what we are to do with our fear. It is upon us like some kind of a vast uneasiness, a tormenting dread. We are all afraid! We're afraid of what another war would bring, a war of atomic energy in the hands of the angry hordes of Asia. No use to lightly attempt to get rid of it. No use to say: "Begone foolish fear." It is NOT foolish fear! The problem is not how to get rid of it, but how, properly, to use it. We can let it frighten us back into isolationism. Some are urging that. We can let it divide us and set us quarreling among ourselves. We can let it start us down the road to witch hunts and mass hysteria. We are a highly emotional people. We do things in huge proportions. As someone has said: "When the news is good, we go to sleep; when it is bad, we go to pieces."

We must not let fear overleap its purpose in pathological manifestations. We must make it a friend. Let it lead us to repentance, spur us to righteousness and redemption. We must see God working in and through our fear.

Dr. Stanley Durkee tells a story of a storm at sea. It was one of those raging, violent storms that sweep occasionally over the North Atlantic in the winter months. The great ship was laboring heavily, her engines holding her into the teeth of the howling gale that played with a ship like she was a toy on the ocean. So long had the storm lasted that the passengers' nerves were beginning to give way. Huddled in the salon, unable to

sleep they wept and prayed, unnerved people fearing
that the ship would be beaten to pieces under the
pounding of the waves.

Then suddenly, the captain stood in the doorway,
called there to prevent what might have become a panic.
A strong, confident, weathered seaman with a kindly
face, he walked to the center of the room and talked
quietly to them. He told them of the storms that he and
his ship had already passed through. He told them that
the engines were working perfectly and that there was
no evidence of dangerous strain anywhere on the ship.
Calmly, masterfully, in a voice vibrant with emotion, he
said: "We will trust in God and in our good ship, and God
will bring us through." The people strangely grew quiet,
almost brave again. They had looked into the face of a
captain who honored the Master of the sea, and their
fears were gone.

Do you suppose that we could do that now? There is
no greater need across the whole earth today than if we
take a look into the face of the Captain again, a long, good
look. Then we will know that He is still the Master of
life's turbulent sea; and fear -- the fear that overshoots
its mark -- will be gone.

Why are we afraid? There are many good reasons,
and they will force us to turn to the Master. Where else?

When Your Mouth's in the Dust

"It is good that one should wait quietly for the salvation of the Lord. It is good for a man that he bear the yoke in his youth. Let him sit alone in silence, when he has laid it on him; let him put his mouth in the dust -- there may yet be hope; let him give his cheek to the smiter, and be filled with insults. For the Lord will not cast off forever, but, though he cause grief, he will have compassion according to the abundance of his steadfast love; for he does not willingly afflict or grieve the sons of men."
(Lamentations 3:26-33 RSV)

*****

Arthur John Gossip was one of the greats of the great Scottish preachers. The first sermon that he preached after his wife's bewildering and untimely death was entitled: "But When Life Tumbles In, What Then?" Among other things, he said: "I cannot comprehend how people in trouble and loss and bereavement can fling away peevishly from the Christian faith. In God's name, fling away to what? Have we not lost enough without losing that, too? You people in sunshine MAY believe the faith, but we in the shadow MUST believe it."

An old minister was speaking to a class of seminary students. Said he: "Never preach a sermon without some word of comfort for the sorrowing. There is always someone there with a heavy heart." That's true. Trouble is a universal experience. No man, living or dead, has ever completely escaped it.

Ella Wheeler Wilcox wrote:

"Laugh, and the world laughs with you;
Weep, and you weep alone;
For the sad old earth must borrow its mirth,
But has trouble enough of its own."

The unfortunate thing is that there are times when laughter is both incongruous and impossible. Life begins in pain and ends in pain; and between birth and death, there is no end of trouble.

What do we do when life tumbles in? For Shakespeare had it right when he said: "When sorrows come, they come not in single spies, but in battalions."

Surely Christianity has something to say here. The symbol of its faith is a cross. Buddhism has no cross. Laughing Buddhas seldom bother with the problem of trouble. They seek to escape from life, and the sooner the better. Christianity's word is not to escape, but to endure.

The first word, obviously, is that we must face trouble. We are not saying that we should LIKE it -- just face it. We need not deny it, as some do, saying that all pain is an "error of the mortal minds." To be sure, when you have a severe pain in the body, you have a pain in the mind, too. But pain is not an error; it is a warning. There is something wrong with the body, and the brain is telling us about it.

Someone spawned this limerick for those who deny the reality of pain:

"There was a faith healer in Deal
Who said, 'Although pain is not real,

If I sit on a pin
And it punctures my skin,
I dislike what I fancy I feel.' "

Others seek to evade tackling the problem of trouble. They consider morbid anything that deals with suffering.

One time a parishioner was in the hospital and underwent a particularly painful type of surgery. He complained to me that his son, who lived in the same city, had never been in the hospital to visit him. So I called the son and asked him for the cause of his neglect. He gave me the excuse that people usually give for not visiting hospitals -- and there are many who don't -- "I just can't stand to see anyone suffer." Dig a little deeper, as I did in that case, and you find that the real reason is that some people don't want to be reminded that suffering is part of the common lot of mankind, and that they, also, might be called upon to suffer. They just don't want to face that, as though staying away from the hospital is going to get rid of the suffering that goes on there.

Some people did not like the motion picture "M*A*S*H" and their reason for not liking it was interesting to me. Most of them that I talked to did not object to the flagrant immorality, the nudity, the profanity, nor the obvious sacrilege in the picture. They were repulsed by the portrayal of the scenes in the operating tent of the battlefield hospital -- the horror of the blood, the gore, the terribly maiméd bodies, the pain, and the sudden death. To anyone who had witnessed such scenes in real life, if anything, the film portrayal was understated. But people cannot bear to see, even in a picture, what some of their countrymen must endure in reality. At all costs, they must avoid facing the existence of such human trouble.

Hosts of people rebel against God because of their troubles. Many of our superficial attitudes toward trouble come from our inadequate concepts of God. Pascal once wrote that "it is the pathetic fate of God to be everlastingly misunderstood." Rather than a God revealed in the life of Jesus, people often make God a fiend. An embittered father who had lost three sons in the war was thoroughly convinced that God had murdered his sons. I remember a personal friend, whose wife was killed in an automobile accident while he was driving. Though he was a faithful church member, he gave up Christianity completely. He became almost a recluse, and he constantly, publicly, cursed God for killing the woman he loved.

I remember making a death call, and the daughter of the deceased man screamed at me as I walked into the house: "What are YOU doing HERE? You don't think we're going to believe in God anymore, after He let Daddy die!"

Let me hasten to say that if I believed in a God who deliberately visited floods and wars and pestilence upon His people, I would join the blasphemers. Such a God is false and deserves to be condemned. He is NOT the Father of our Lord Jesus Christ. He is not a Father at all. He is a fiend.

We come to an intelligent understanding of trouble only as we understand the purposes of God. Could He make us as finite creatures with bodies and brains, without physical and mental suffering? Bodies like ours are subject to wear and tear with the passing years. It's impossible to conceive of physical life as we have it, from birth to death, without suffering. Had God made us as disembodied spirits to inhabit the earth, He could have eliminated suffering. But according to His purposes, He has given us babies to love and caress, families in which to live physically, husbands and wives to comfort and to love. Given bodies that work and minds that think, trouble is inevitable.

Furthermore, we must consider the fact that we bring much of our trouble upon ourselves. During wartime, there is always some pious soul who shouts: "Why doesn't God stop the war?" The fact is that stopping wars is not according to His purposes. He made us with freedom to live at peace or at war as we choose. He yearns for a family of obedient sons and daughters, with characters akin to His own. He could have made us robots; then there would have been no wars. There would also have been no character. It's difficult for us to understand that much of the trouble that we experience is self-imposed. We are never very quick to shoulder our own responsibilities. I have known men who have gambled away and drunk away or played away their fortunes, and then they blamed God for their economic plight. Others, endowed with healthy bodies, abuse them by breaking every one of the known rules of health; and then they blame God when illness strikes.

Dr. George Buttrick says: "If there is a tenement fire and lives are lost, (1) someone was careless with matches or cigarettes, (2) the landlord may have sought excessive profits, (3) someone broke the law concerning fire hazards. God was NOT burning up some of His children!" God's laws concerning sowing and reaping holds true, not only in agriculture, but in the lives of men. Blaming God for our own irresponsible acts is sheer stupidity.

Furthermore, while we cannot understand all trouble, and it is perfectly natural that we should turn against it, this fact is incontrovertible, there is no PROGRESS without it. The testimony of history is that progress is always through suffering. The water current downstream makes for the sturdy salmon. The stiff air currents and the inaccessible cliffs make for the strong eagle. Strength comes from the conquest of something that resists us.

The more sensitive the life, the higher the capacity to climb. When God put an oyster in the ocean bed, He gave it almost no sensitivity. When it is hungry, it merely opens its shell for whatever food the water around it may contain. When it is satisfied, it closes its shell. That's about all you can say about an oyster, unless you enjoy eating them. When God made man, He put the sensitive nerves on the outside of the skeleton. Man's sensitivity to hunger goaded him into cultivating the fields and providing a more abundant harvest. His sensitivity to cold and heat prompted him to make clothes and to build houses. Man's necessities made him both father and mother of many inventions.

Take away man's wants, and you take away his worth. Take away his thirst for knowledge, and you close the schools, libraries and laboratories of the world. Take his desire for comfort from him, and you stop scientific research in a thousand fields. The greater the man's sensitivity to trouble, the higher he climbs in the conquest of it. This is the history of the human family. Take trouble out of the world, and you take away a large chunk of its progress.

We all know, for instance, that patience is a great virtue, but how could you develop great patience without great pain? If there were no fight to life, there would be no fortitude. If there were no suffering, there would be no highly developed sense of sympathy. We may seek comfort, but God's purpose for us is character. It is impossible to conceive of character without the virtues of patience and fortitude and sympathetic understanding. It could be that character and trouble go together like love and marriage, and horse and carriage.

On the wall of a hospital some unknown sufferer wrote a poem. He would have been famous, if he had signed his name. But, no matter, the poem speaks for itself. Listen:
> "The cry of man's anguish went up to God,
>> 'Lord, take away pain
>> The shadow that darkens the world thou hast
>>> made
>> The close coiling chain
> That strangles the heart, the burden that weighs
> On the wings that would soar --
> Lord, take away pain from the world thou hast
>> made
> That it love Thee the more.'

Then answered the Lord to the cry of the world,
  'Shall I take away pain,
  And with it the power of the soul to endure,
  Made strong by the strain?
Shall I take away pity that knits heart to heart,
And sacrifice high?
Will you lose all your heroes that lift from the fire
  White brows to the sky?
    Shall I take away love that redeems with a
      price,
    And smiles with its loss?
Can ye spare from your lives that would cling unto
  mine
The Christ on His Cross?' "

Trouble must be faced. Trouble must be intelligently understood according to the purposes of God. Troubles must be used creatively. Oh, you can rail against trouble, and rebel against God, or you can accept trouble with the attitude of the stoic that "I will suffer through it." Or you can USE trouble, as Jesus did, who transformed the ghastly cross into a glorious crown. There is another strange thing that we should say, that TROUBLE IS A TRUST. God has given us birth in a sea of trouble, trusting that we use it creatively.

J. Wallace Hamilton tells the story of the letter he received from a sister in Africa. She was the wife of a missionary. They had lost their nine-year-old son by tragic death. Just one line in that letter told a great story about two great souls. Here is the line: "God has trusted us with great sorrow." Think of all the patience, all of the trust, all of the confidence, all of the love that those parents must have had to write that one sentence: "God has trusted us with a great sorrow."

I remember a couple in Chicago in the days before the Salk Vaccine. Their son was struck down by bulbar polio, and he died after a few agonizing days in an iron lung. He was eighteen years old and their only child, and the hurt and the shock went deep. But I will always remember what they said to me after the funeral service: "We thank God that He gave us eighteen wonderful years with our boy." The angels must have rejoiced at that heroic response to such tragedy.

Trouble is a teacher, if we but listen. God tells us how to handle it. It need not wedge us away from God. It can lead us into His arms.

> "Go ask the infidel, what boon he brings us,
> What charm for aching heart he can reveal,
> Sweet as that heavenly promise Hope sings us --
> 'Earth has no sorrow that God cannot heal.' "

Ask Ole Bull, the Norwegian violinist, one of the most fascinating characters in the musical world. One evening, while giving a concert in the Opera House at Paris, the A string on his violin broke. He calmly shifted the difficult composition to another key and finished it on three strings. Had I had the privilege of hearing that great violinist just one time, I would have chosen that night. When calamity befell him, it was a test of his mastery to bring the composition to a glorious finish without a flaw.

I don't know all the troubles you are confronting. Some of them, I know. I don't know the troubles you have confronted or that you will confront. I only know that they will be a part of your life. I know, with absolute certainty, that all of us will be put to the test before our days here on earth are finished. Of this we can be sure. What counts is not what troubles do to us, but what we do with the troubles.

Lord Byron, for instance, and Sir Walter Scott were both lame. Byron was so embittered by his lameness and he brooded about it until he utterly loathed his lame leg. Every time he went into a public place, he was conscious of people looking at him. On the other hand, Scott never complained or spoke one bitter word about his disability, not even, they tell us, to his dearest friends. They never heard him mention it. The real question is not the severity of the trouble, but it's in our attitude toward it, and how different those attitudes can be in differing people.

General William Booth, the founder of the Salvation Army, went blind. His son, Bramwell, had to tell the old soldier of the cross that his blindness was incurable and permanent. And so said General Booth: "I have done what I could for God and for the people with my eyes, and now I will do what I can for God and the people without my eyes."

Trouble can be terrifying. It can also be triumphant.

"When your mouth is in the dust -- wait and hope in the Lord."

The Lonesome Road

"And there he came to a cave, and lodged there; and behold, the word of the Lord came to him, and he said to him, 'What are you doing here, Elijah?' He said, 'I have been very jealous for the Lord, the God of hosts; for the people of Israel have forsaken thy covenant, thrown down thy altars, and slain thy prophets with the sword; and I, even I only, am left; and they seek my life, to take it away.' And he said, 'Go forth, and stand upon the mount before the Lord.' And behold, the Lord passed by, and a great and strong wind rent the mountains, and broke in pieces the rocks before the Lord, but the Lord was not in the wind; and after the wind an earthquake, but the Lord was not in the earthquake."

(I Kings 19:9-11 RSV)

*****

The tired, old cliche comes so easily to our lips. We are always ready to spout it at a moment's notice, it seems. For instance, our friend is in trouble with a terrible weight heavy upon him. Our friend lies in a hospital bed, convulsed by pain and facing emergency surgery. Our friend is facing a crisis in his life, the outcome of which may change his whole future, and we trot out the cliche, ready for instant use.

You remember it. You've used it often enough. "I know just how you feel." Guilty? Of course you are. We are all guilty of using that cliche: "I know just how you feel." At its best, it's a useless, stupid statement, and at its worst, it is an outright lie. The truth is that we DON'T know how our friend feels at all.

In his trouble or pain or crisis, he is traveling one of the lonesome roads of life. We simply cannot know how he feels, because his problem has separated him from all humanity. We cannot share his feelings. We cannot understand his emotions. We cannot fully identify with him. He walks alone. Sometimes life seems to be made up of lonely roads and the world filled with lonely people.

The part of the narrative of the life of Elijah is typical of many of the lonesome people of our world. Here we see him crouching in the cave, feeling that he is utterly forsaken, that all of his supporters have been slain, and he has been threatened with death by Jezebel. How many of us crouch in the caves of life or in the dark corners of human existence or in the closets of our own solitude and weep with Elijah? And even after God has made His presence known and His help assured to Elijah by the great wind, the earthquake and the fire and, most important, a still small voice, he still says: "I, even I only, am left, and they seek my life, to take it away."

It is a very human cry expressed most graphically by our own Lord Jesus Christ in His own humanity when He cries out from the cross: "My God, my God, why have YOU forsaken me?"

Loneliness takes many shapes and manifests itself in a variety of ways. The girl who sat in my study had asked to see me immediately. She was a rather ordinary, pleasant-looking girl. She blurted out her story. She had come from a small, rural community a few months before, to work in one of the offices in our city. Now she was pregnant with the child of a married man who worked in her office. How had it happened to this well-raised girl with strong church and family ties? She put it quite simply: "When I came here, I was terribly, terribly lonely, and he was kind to me." But now the tragedy was that instead of dispelling her loneliness, she would have to walk one of the loneliest roads of all -- the road of the unwed mother.

Some time ago, the papers carried a story of an elderly couple, who were found dead in their tiny apartment in another city. The woman had written a note, stating that they did not have enough money to care for their necessities, and no one seemed to care for them anymore, and they had decided to escape their poverty and loneliness by taking their own lives.

There are many lonely roads in life. A doctor tells of a weekly visit he made to an elderly lady for what she assured him was a very necessary check-up each week. He finally diagnosed her trouble as loneliness. She had no relatives and very few friends, and she was perfectly willing to pay the doctor's fee in order to have someone to talk to each week, someone who was concerned about her welfare. It was her way of escaping the fear of loneliness.

In another parish, an aged man left a large sum of money to the church, with the church's assurance that they would look after his unmarried daughter, who was supposedly dying of a fatal chronic disease. After his death, the church kept its promise, only they found that the only disease from which the daughter was suffering was loneliness. She rallied and she lived for years. The father had known her problem, and he was insuring the fact that someone would always take an interest in her after he was gone.

Recently a girl of sixteen was admitted to a California State Hospital for the mentally retarded. That she should be in such an institution was adequately demonstrated by the fact that she tested to have an Intelligence Quotient of 50, about half what we would expect the normal person to have. After a thorough study of the case, the word went out that she should be treated with firmness, but also with patience and kindness, regardless of what she did. Well, for three months, she screamed and scratched and bit and kicked her way around the hospital, with no retaliation from anyone except to restrain her when she became too violent or too abusive. She was not ignored or merely tolerated. She was given mature love.

And then a remarkable thing happened. Apparently, convinced of the genuineness of the attitude of the adults about her, she relaxed. Her hostile attitude made a complete about-face. Within a few weeks, she was given a second test by the psychologist and that showed that she had an Intelligence Quotient of 130. Her intelligence had not jumped 80 points just because she was in the hospital. The girl had the same intelligence when she came into the hospital as she did when she was retested. The secret of the change was that for the first time in her life, as her case study showed, she had friends whom, she was convinced, CARED about her. She had entered the hospital as a psychologically lonely person. She was one who was completely isolated from all of society.

There are many lonely roads in life. Every human being may struggle with one or more of them.

There is the lonesome road of homesickness. Have you ever been really homesick? May I tell you that it's a rather devastating feeling. I remember the experience in Japan after the war. I had not been home for over two years. At night as I walked down the streets of a Japanese village and saw the families gathered around their evening meal, I envied those poverty-stricken and defeated people. I envied them because at least they were at home, and they were together. I felt like the loneliest person in the world.

One evening a man dropped into the church. He said: "I saw your light, and I thought I'd come in for a minute. I'm here for a few weeks on a special job. Each evening at dusk, my family gathers at the table at home, and when I'm away, I get terribly homesick every evening just at dusk. I really don't know what to do with myself."

There is the lonesome road of social ostracism. When people look, act or speak differently from the rest of us, the tendency is to ostracize them from the community life. Without, perhaps, meaning to do so, we apply the social boycott. When one expresses a view contrary to the masses, there is a tendency to alienate him. We Americans teach our children from birth that they should do their own thinking and that they should espouse a case in which they believe, no matter how unpopular. This is the American way.

But lately, we have tried to destroy people whose views differ from our own. We have seen young pastors destroyed, or at least their influence weakened, because of their stand for Christian brotherhood on the race issue. It is difficult to believe that church people who have heard the Bible preached all of their lives can stoop to this kind of condemnation. Sad to say, there are many of them who have done just that.

Sometimes community gossip can play havoc with a person's reputation. The tragedy of tragedies is that there are many good, law-abiding people who will believe the worst about a person, without taking the time to check the sources of information to get to the truth. We need to withhold our judgment until we know the facts.

A woman told me the other day about what her husband had been doing in being unfaithful to her. He had denied it, but she was accepting the evidence of what other people had told her. Without a single shred of evidence which she had received herself, she was ready to break up her marriage on the basis of rumor spread by gossiping people.

One teenager took her own life because of a rumor

spread by her neighbor that she had come home at daylight in a drunken stupor, her clothes disheveled, delivered to her home by a wild young man in a sports car. The facts were that she had stayed all night with her aunt who was very ill, and her cousin had brought her home in the morning.

The road of community censure and social ostracism is a lonely road, indeed.

There is the lonely road of defeat or failure. We Americans are winners by nature. Korea was a bitter pill for us and Vietnam is worse. We always WIN, and that goes in personal relationships, too. We like to win, and we like winners! Almost automatically our attitude changes toward someone who has failed. This happens so imperceptibly that sometimes we scarcely notice it, but it makes it a lonesome road for him.

A man spoke to me who, at one time, was very successful and wealthy. Then things went sour, and he lost everything he had. He said: "You know, I don't mind losing my business or my money. I can make that again. But I didn't know that I'd lose my friends when I lost my fortune. I see people who were my bosom buddies a few months ago, and now they hardly know me when we meet on the street." As anyone knows who has failed in his business or lost his job, it's a lonesome road. It makes it a lonely road for him.

The road of retirement is also a lonesome road. How many a man has received his gold watch and his pension, and then is placed on a shelf and forgotten. No one seems to need him. The world moves too fast for him. It's too busy for him. The number of our retired, elderly people is increasing every day, and we haven't yet found out what to do with them. They are like the old clothes in the attic -- too good to throw away but too old to be of use. What will retirement be like for us? Very often, it's a lonesome road.

Then there is the lonesome road of illness and death. When we are ill, there is a kind of barrier raised between us and other people. We feel cut off from healthy society. We feel out of it. Just as a person who is well can't remember how it felt to be sick, so a person who is sick can't remember how it felt to be well. And so, every healthy and robust person who breezes in to his hospital room is a kind of a threat to him, and as the caller leaves the sick room and dashes away to again be embroiled in the activities of life, the person left behind in the sick bed feels more lonely than ever, more cut off, more shut away. Illness is a lonely road.

What do we do with loneliness? We must face our loneliness and do something about it. It's one thing to know that we are lonely. It's still another thing to face it head on. It is wise to search for the cause. We can handle it better, if we understand its origin. The steps by which freedom from loneliness can come are simple and fairly well accepted. That doesn't mean that they are easy to follow. The very nature of the fear of loneliness makes adjustment difficult. Sometimes harsh discipline of mind and body is necessary. But a vast company of well-adjusted people can testify to victory over loneliness.

THE FIRST STEP IS TO CULVIVATE NORMAL, SOCIAL RELATIONSHIPS. Broaden your circle of acquaintances, deepen your friendships. Although that is not the entire answer to the problem, it certainly is a good step in the right direction. Almost everyone shuns the meeting of people at times. The most expressive extrovert has probably worked at it a long time. You may admire his ability in greeting strangers and mixing with people, without being aware of the fact that he wasn't born that way. There was a time when he, too, was afraid of people and had to force himself, literally, to join the group.

Margaret Lee Runbeck illustrates this very human trait in an incident that she relates about her high school commencement. In being the valedictorian of the class, she was assigned a seat on the platform next to the guest speaker. Her class advisor reminded her that she should carry on a friendly conversation with the guest of honor. This seemed too much, but she tried to do it. She whispered finally: "I'm supposed to talk wittily to you, but I can't think of a thing to say, and I'm scared to death." "I'm scared, too," the speaker replied. "I've got a speech written down here, but I don't think it's very good, and besides . . . " "But you don't have to be afraid," stammered the young girl. "Neither do you," the speaker replied. "I'll tell you a secret and then you'll never need to be scared again. Everbody on earth is shy, self-conscious and unsure of himself. Everybody is timid about meeting strangers. So, if you'll just spend the first minute that you are in the presence of some stranger trying to make HIM feel comfortable, you will never suffer from self-consciousness again. Just try it." She did. And it worked. The speaker for that commencement was at that time, the Assistant Secretary of the Navy. Later, he was elected President of the United States on four occasions. It was Franklin Delano Roosevelt, certainly a man who was adept at making friends.

It is a trite but true saying that you have to be a friend, if you want to have one. If we are willing to pay the price of friendship, to take the initiative, then our friendships will help us overcome our loneliness.

STEP #2 -- A HEALING POWER COMES FROM SERVICE. Multitudes of people have overcome loneliness to a degree by plunging themselves into some worthy cause. Apply to a volunteer bureau, if you want to know the vast number of worthy causes that need workers. The selfish, self-centered life can be a lonely life. The Christian Church offers countless opportunities for service. I have never heard anyone who was involved in the work of a church ever accuse that church of being unfriendly or complain about being lonely in the congregation, as long as he is working in it. Once you are busy with other people working for God and His Kingdom, you forget all about the fact that you were lonely.

STEP #3 -- LEARN TO DELIGHT IN MOMENTS ALONE. The world is a crowded place. There is very little privacy anymore. Modern living makes it difficult to be alone. But it's mentally and spiritually healthy for us to be alone at times. Christ didn't always walk the lonesome road because He was forced to. Sometimes He chose to be alone. The person is never lonely who has learned how to be good company for himself. But that ability depends upon the final and most important step:

APPLY YOUR CHRISTIAN FAITH TO YOUR PROBLEM OF LONELINESS. There is nothing in all the world like our religion to cure the lonely heart. There is no wall high enough, no barrier thick enough that God cannot penetrate it.

I love that scene in "Green Pastures" when the children of Israel have gone on ahead into the Promised Land, and they have left Moses behind on Mount Pisgah on the other side of Jordan. What a pitifully lonely figure he is as he watches them go, and what a terrible lonesomeness descends upon him. Then he hears a movement behind him, and he feels a hand on his shoulder. He asks: "Is you wid me, Lord?" The voice that comes back warms his soul: "Cou'se I is, Moses. Cou'se I is."

Jesus walked our lonesome road. He knew heartache and tears. He knew rejection and ostracism. He knew the loneliness that comes from standing alone for a great cause. He knew defeat and fatigue. He understood life as we face it. He knew the answers. He found that He had company on the lonesome road. He found the Father with Him on the lonesome road. He spoke those comforting words from which every lonely person can take heart: "I am not alone, because the Father is with me."

We need never walk alone, because He has said: "I am with you alway."

80

80

80

The Faith of the Foolish

"He destined us in love to be his sons through Jesus Christ, according to the purpose of his will, to the praise of his glorious grace which he freely bestowed on us in the Beloved. In him we have redemption through his blood, the forgiveness of our trespasses, according to the riches of his grace which he lavished upon us."

(Ephesians 1:5-8 RSV)

*****

Last Lord's Day when I finished my sermon, I really stopped in the middle. I left it as a kind of dangling participle, an unresolved chord. Happily, one young man leaving the church said to me: "I appreciated your sermon, Pastor. When do we hear the rest of it?" I was grateful for his perceptiveness. Last Lord's Day, you remember, I spoke about the judgment of God working throughout the centuries of history, that God, in His own time, destroys those things in humanity that He cannot tolerate. And, indeed, if this were not true, the Church of Jesus Christ would not exist today.

But now, having spoken of the law and the judgment of God, let me lapse into some foolishness. I'm going to speak of the Gospel, and that, to many of us, as the Bible says, is unmitigated tomfoolery. Let's make it very clear that no educated, scientifically-oriented or socially sophisticated person is EXPECTED to BELIEVE what I am about to talk about, because I am going to talk about the love of God and the foolishness of the Gospel.

The strange thing is that the Bible makes this foolishness perfectly evident. The Word makes it very clear that to the world and to the man who is part of the world, the Gospel of the Cross of Jesus Christ is ridiculous, asinine, idiotic, or even insane. It flies in the face of everything that we think is fair, just or reasonable. In plain words, IT JUST DOESN'T MAKE SENSE!

Paul says, however: "The foolishness of God is wiser than the wisdom of men." And Paul was a wise man. Again he writes: "Where is the philosopher? Where is the scholar? Where is the debater of the issue? Has not the nonsense and folly of the world been shown up by God?" And certainly, if it hadn't been shown up in Paul's day, it certainly has been shown up in our day.

Here we are historically, perhaps, facing the most grave crisis in the world that we have ever faced, and it affects every facet of our existence here on this globe. And yet, there isn't a single, solitary soul who knows a tinker's damn about what we can do to alleviate this crisis. I don't care who they are, how brilliant, how many degrees they have after their names, they DON'T KNOW!

Someone has asked: "What is the most difficult task of a pastor?" And I often reply: "It is to explain to people the grace of God." I often feel like the country preacher who said: "I am going to try to unscrew the inscrutable." And that's what we feel like doing when we talk about the grace of God. What is God's grace? I tell my confirmands that we call a certain note in music a "grace" note, because that measure of music DOES NOT DESERVE that note, but it is given it. I tell them that when their teacher says: "I will give you 'a day of grace' to get your assignment in," that is a day that they DO NOT DESERVE. I tell them that we call the prayer that we often say before meals "grace," because we are acknowledging the fact that we DO NOT DESERVE the gifts that are set before us.

But all of this does not define it. All of this is like describing the Grand Canyon by saying: "Well, it's a hole in the ground." Who can describe it? Who can define it? Who can draw any human similies that even come close to allowing us to understand what God's grace really is? Here is a word that is used 170 times in the New Testament; and yet, we can't define it. We can't explain it. We don't really know what it is. We listen to that beautiful hymn:

> "Amazing grace, how sweet the sound
> That saved a wretch like me.
> I once was lost, but now I'm found,
> Was blind, but now I see."

But we don't see. Yes, God has given us minds to reason with, and we are to use our minds to the utmost of their capacity. But there are a host of things in the world that we don't understand, and the most strange and surprising and inexplicable of all of them is the grace of God. It isn't rational. It isn't logical. It isn't just. (At least not what we think of as justice). It isn't human. We can't come close to expressing it in our own lives. As John says: "While the law came through Moses, GRACE and truth came by Jesus Christ." We can, however, only understand what being a Christian is (if we at least understand a little bit about grace, for being a Christian is not doing this or doing that or some other thing). Being a Christian is ACCEPTING the GRACE OF GOD.

That means, also, understanding sin in its most profound sense. Oh, when we talk about sin, we aren't talking about little naughtiness or the outward breaking of the Ten Commandments, or we aren't talking about sex. Most of the time, when you talk about sin, people think you're talking about sex. It's none of these things. SIN IS TURNING ONE'S BACK ON GOD, not just a momentary lapse in the rules of the house or a season of indiscretion. IT IS THE REJECTION OF GOD THE FATHER in His Person, the spurning of God's grace and love. It is shaking our puny little fist to heaven. It is spitting at the skies.

Like the father who instructed his son to drive very carefully and at a low speed when he drove his little sister to the grocery. The son laughs in the father's face and calls him an old fogy and takes off in a cloud of dust. A few moments later, there is a tragic accident, and the little sister is killed, but the son is still alive and unhurt. And now, he must come back and face the father. This is what sin is. And the father waits with forgiveness. That is grace!

Here is where God's grace is so radical. That is, God forgives WITHOUT it being CONDITIONAL. How often we say: "I'll forgive you, if . . . " "I'll forgive you, if you do so and so." Our forgiveness is always conditioned on certain things that the other person does. God's grace is UNconditional. Also, men forgive things when sin is not conscious or deliberate. God forgives man no matter if it was fully intended and premeditated. Men forgive because they need to have back the person that they have forgiven, but God has no dependency upon the one loved. Men forgive because they see themselves as sinners and they see themselves in the acts of others, but God needs no such tolerance, because He is holy. It is clear God's forgiveness is not an act of justice. It is an act of LOVE. Don't try to ever make justice out of Christianity, it doesn't work. Don't ever try to make it a tit for tat. It doesn't work. That's why we can't understand it.

Some of the states are voting laws reinstating, they hope, under constitutional provisions, the death penalty for certain crimes. Someone handed me a letter to the editor, which I missed in our own papers: "Do Things God's Way," the headline is, "Execute Killers." And the letter goes on: "All Bible-believing" -- oh, how they LOVE to use that word -- "All Bible-believing Christians in Iowa should get behind the efforts of Attorney General Richard Turner to reinstate the death penalty for willful murder. In the holy Scripture God commands that all murderers be put to death." THAT IS A DAMNED LIE! And this is a Bible-believing Christian!

What was God's answer to the sin, even of murder among His people? To allow them to murder His own Son, that was His answer. That is grace. You say that makes God's forgiveness too easy? Then, again, you don't know anything about Christianity. You don't know the enormity of our sin until you experience God's grace. God's grace, the Gospel. To the Jews, a stumbling block, because they wanted the law by which they could push each other around. To the Greeks, it was foolishness, because they were intellectual, and this wasn't intellectual.

I was counseling with a woman whose husband had run away with another woman and stayed for about three months, and then, out of the blue, he called her and asked to come back to her and the children, begged her forgiveness. She called me to ask what she should do about it. I said: "Do you love your husband?" "Yes." I said: "That's your answer. As God loves you." She said: "I know what all my neighbors and all the ladies on my block will say: 'Are you going to let him just walk back like that?'" "If they say that," I told her, "tell them to take out their Bibles, if they have one, and turn to the 15th Chapter of St. Luke and read the story of the Prodigal Son. That will give them their answer." A man who had disgraced his father in every way that was possible, and yet, his father opened his arms in forgiveness and love.

God's love doesn't depend on our penitence, either. Sometimes we think we have to put on a good crying jag to prove to God that we're really sorry for our sins. No. God loves us at the height of our rebellionn. Even as we blasphemed Him, He loves us. As Luther said: "Sometimes there are no people closer or dearer to God's heart than those who deny Him most vehemently." It doesn't depend on our penitence. "While we were yet sinners, Christ died for us." Most of us don't understand Christianity, and that's why we don't understand grace.

Let's start out by saying that, first, Christianity is not a religion. Don't come around and talk to me about religion, if you want to talk about Christianity. Christianity is not a religion. Religions begin with men. Christianity is the revelation of God. It's not a religion. It was thrust upon us by the love of God, whether we wanted it or not. It was revealed to us, whether we were ready for it or not. We didn't go looking for it. Some would say that religion is man's search for God. What a bunch of nonsense! No man searches for God. All we, like Adam, run away from Him. Christianity is not a relative. We don't set it alongside the other world's so-called religions and say: "Now, which is the best?" Christianity doesn't fit. It would be utter presumption for us to carry on our Foreign Mission work, if we didn't realize we were carrying the truth and the life in the revelation of Jesus Christ. Christianity is a place where the ways part. You either are or you are not, and Christianity is completely intolerant. We don't come around and say: "Now, we're all going to the same place. We just worship God in a different way." You find that for me in the Bible. Find that for me in the words of Jesus Christ, who says: "I am the way, the truth, and the life, and NO MAN COMETH UNTO THE FATHER BUT BY ME."

And so the question always is in the end: "What do you think of Christ?" That's what He asked the people. That's what He asked the Pharisees. And He wanted to indicate that their day of disputation and fooling around with the law was over, that the question: "What think ye of Christ and the grace of God that He has brought?" is the real question of our day. It sweeps away all of our religious intellectualism, like this rash of articles and books, "My Search for God." Most of our religious intellectualism is a sublimation of our guilt or a way we want to inflate our scholarly egotism. As one great theologian said: "If God could be discovered, God would be destroyed." But He doesn't allow us that privilege.

Edward Arlington Robinson says that he has the word for our time: "The world is a kindergarten in which millions of bewildered infants are trying to spell 'God' with the wrong blocks." God cannot be spelled in blocks of logic, because He is not a theorem to be proved. You ask me to prove the existence of God to you? I don't have to. You already KNOW, despite all of your lies and evasions. You need no proof that He is there. Man does not search for God, he flees.

Francis Thompson in his "Hound of Heaven" was not writing just for himself. He was writing for all of us in our human experience when he said:

"I fled Him, down the nights
    and down the days;
I fled Him, down the arches of the
    years;
I fled Him, down the labyrinthine
    ways
Of my own mind; and in the mist
    of tears
I hid from Him, and under running
    laughter.
Up vistaied hopes I sped;
    And shot, precipitated,
Adown Titanic glooms of chasmed
    fears,
From those strong feet that
    followed,
    Followed after.
    But with unhurrying chase,
    And unperturbed pace,
Deliberate speed, majestic instancy,

They beat -- and a Voice beat
More instant than the Feet --
'All things betray thee,
Who betrayest Me.' "
We are NOT searching for God. He is searching for us!

Is Christianity an escape from life, an easy way out? Oh, beloved, a faith that begins on a blood-splattered cross is not an escape from life. This is the facing of real evil by a real God. The cross means that we must face reality. The cross is God confronting us in life with His grace, not a God standing around whispering words of encouragement or self-improvement, not offering bribes if we are only good children, but a God who chooses, condemns, redeems, pardons and LOVES.

I recently spoke to a group of Alcoholics Anonymous. They were there, not because they wanted to be. They were there by court order. The leader of the group told me: "You're going to be talking, Pastor, to a lot of men who have no religious life or conviction whatsoever. We in AA, as I am an AA member," he said, "know that unless we turn our lives into God's hands, we can't beat this disease." So what did I speak to these men about? The grace of God, the grace of God that could save them, redeem them, and restore them to life once more, the strength and the power of His Holy Spirit that would give them the ability to overcome their malady. After my address, several of the men remained to chat, at which the Director was quite surprised. But the last man who stayed said: "Look at me, Pastor. You couldn't guess my age, because I'm a lot, lot younger than I look. All I can say is that if God can forgive me, He can forgive anyone in the world."

And as each of us looks at himself, may we say to ourselves: "If God can forgive ME, He can forgive anyone else in the world," for by Jesus Christ came grace.

"In Him we have redemption through His blood . . . according to the riches of His grace which He lavished upon us."

The Fence Builders

"For He is our peace, who has made us both one, and has broken down the dividing wall of hostility . . . So then you are no longer strangers and sojourners, but you are fellow citizens with the saints and members of the household of God, built upon the foundation of the apostles and prophets, Christ Jesus Himself being the cornerstone, in whom the whole structure is joined together and grows into a holy temple in the Lord; in whom you also are built into it for a dwelling place of God in the Spirit."

(Ephesians 2:14 and 19-22 RSV)

*****

One day I was looking for a piece of railing for our home, and that search took me to the fence department of the store in which I was shopping, and there I saw the card hanging with the old proverb printed on it: "Good fences make good neighbors." And, mentally, I had to shake my head in wonder at how, with the kind of redundant repetition, we can make a bit of human stupidity sound like human wisdom. It's perfectly obvious that the TRUTH is that good fences DON'T make good neighbors. Fences are the proof that we can't BE good neighbors.

In Canterbury one summer, the first thing that they showed us was part of the history of that failure. When the Romans brought Western civilization to England in 43 A.D., the first thing they did in laying out the City of Canterbury was to build the wall. And that is the story of mankind: walls around our cities, walls around our castles, walls between nations, stockades around our first settlements. And then, fences, fences everywhere -- around houses, even around our cemeteries. (I was never quite able to decide whether that was to keep the dead in or the living out.)

Back 210 years before Christ, they built one of the wonders of the ancient world, the Great Wall of China. Twenty feet high, thirteen feet wide at the top, it stretched over mountains and valleys and hills for some fourteen hundred miles. There was a guard tower every hundred yards. But that wall was completely useless. It was crossed again and again. Why? Because the guards could be bribed.

France built one of the great fences of all time before World War II. They called it the "Maginot Line." It was promptly flanked and overrun in a few days. The Germans built what they called the "Siegfried Line." It was pulverized by the Allies.

The Communists built the Berlin Wall. It didn't bring security. It brought world-wide shame. But having built it, they couldn't show the world what damned fools they were by taking it down again, and so it still stands there to mock them. They must keep the workers IN the Worker's Paradise, instead of keeping the enemies out.

And, of course, we had to join the company of fools. Have you forgotten the "MacNamara Line" -- the fence that we were going to build completely across Vietnam? It was doomed in the very beginning to be the same kind of failure as all the rest. The Marines who were constantly pounded over that fence reminded us that keeping our fences mended after they were built is not always so easy. So we, like the rest of the fence builders in history, became the laughingstock of the world.

Of course, we have our other fences -- the fence of some four thousand nuclear missiles pointed at every target in the Communist world, just as theirs are pointed at us, along with the antiballistic missiles, and soon we will start on our anti-antiballistic missiles. We already have enough to kill every man, woman and child in the world one hundred times over, but still the insanity goes on.

Obviously, we have strong fences right here in this country. It was fences that split our cities and built our ghettos. Again and again, we are reminded that that is not a river than runs down the middle of our city. That's a fence. "Lee Township against the world," and all of that. How did we create the ghettos? It was quite simple. We built fences based on the myth that the sale of property to members of minority groups devalues the property and the whole community around it. We implemented it by selling to Negroes only in ghettos or fringe areas -- a practice that is still followed pretty much today. Nice, neat, invisible fences!

We have a polite term for another fence that we have built. We call it "the generation gap." Actually, it's a fence, on the one hand, built out of the fear-ridden and change-resisting mentalities of a middle-aged generation who would fence out a much-needed revolution from the minds of their own children. On the other hand, it is built by an overprivileged and undermatured generation of young people who would fence out all of the evidences of accomplishment by the generation before them, which provides the climate in which any revolution can take place.

For instance, to the great majority of our youth, racial brotherhood was not something to argue about as it was among us. It simply IS! Recently, in Durhan, North Caroline, fifty Negro families were moved into a new apartment complex in a white neighborhood. Among the white residents, there was a great uproar and upheavel -- all except among the Duke University students, the married students who lived in two hundred and twenty-five apartments across the street. They knew that, obviously, this sort of thing was necessary; and so they went on with their work unconcerned.

War is another fence. Surveys indicate, whether through the press of all of the campuses of the country or by any other observers, an overwhelming rejection by youth of the United States' policy militarily, a revolution against military conscription and the traditional military training in the ROTC, as all being asinine and ineffective in a missile age. Most of the students are NOT pacifists in the real sense of the term, but the comments heard about the stupidity of our being involved in the war in Southeast Asia are certainly not repeatable from this pulpit.

Another fence is religion. The widespread rejection of institutional religion and the withdrawal from the church by many of our youth stems from their outrage, not only over race and the lily-white churches, but over the brutality of war as it is fought by Christians. They are especially repelled when such killing is glorified as a godly act of patriotism. You see, they don't believe that everything that the United States does is right in the sight of God, and that He blesses us in it because we are God's children. They don't believe that the business of the Christian church is killing Communists. THEY DON'T BELIEVE IT, and they think that we're a bunch of hypocrites!

But just a moment, just a moment. On the other hand, may I introduce the youth to some people whom their fences -- THEIR fences -- have not allowed them to really see or appreciate -- the two most accomplished generations in the history of the world -- their parents and their grandparents. And may I remind the youth, these are the people who within the last five decades have, by their hard work, increased your life expectancy by approximately 50%, and who, while cutting the working days a third, have more than doubled the per capita output. They are the people who have given you a much healthier world than they found themselves. And because of this, you no longer have to fear the terrible epidemics of flu, typhus, diptheria, smallpox, scarlet fever, measles and mumps that they knew in their youth and most of which might have killed them. Dreaded polio is no longer a threat to cripple YOU, my dear young person, for the rest of your life in your youth, and tuberculosis is almost unheard of.

Let me remind you that these remarkable people lived through the greatest depression in all of history. Many of them know what you don't know, what it is to be really poor. Many of them know what it is to be hungry and cold. And because of this, they determined that this would not happen to you. And because they struggled for and gave you the best, you call them materialists. But you are still the tallest, healthiest, brightest and best-looking generation that has ever inhabited the earth, because of THEIR sweat and THEIR concern. And because of them, you will work fewer hours, you will learn more, you will have more leisure time, you will travel to more distant places, and you will have more of a chance to follow your life's ambition.

These are the people who defeated the tyranny of Hitler and Tojo and who, when it was all over, had the Christian compassion to spend billions of dollars to help their former enemies rebuild their homeland, until today Japan and Germany are among the wealthiest nations on earth. And these are the people who had the sense, the good sense, to begin the United Nations. It was these two generations, who through the highest courts of the land, fought racial discrimination. Not the youth, but the parents and grandparents of this country, fought racial discrimination through every turn to bring about a new era of civil rights. They built thousands of expensive high schools for you, and they made higher education a very real possibility for millions, and not just the dream of a wealthy few. They also made a start, albeit a late start, in dealing with pollution and destruction of the environment, not thinking of themselves, but of you and the generations to come. Yes, they had some failures. They didn't find an alternative to war or to racial hate, but they tried, and they are still trying.

Oh, don't you see, young people, and don't you see, adults, the kind of fences that we have erected against each other, so that we cannot really see each other?

But the fences which exist on a global scale, a national scale, a community scale, are most common on the personal level. May I identify a few? I could point out to you a dozen places in our community where families have lived as neighbors for years, and they have not spoken to each other for months. There are high fences in Des Moines, which have been erected out of spite and paid for with hate.

I know members of families of this congregation, brothers and sisters, who haven't spoken to each other since their parents died and the will was probated. I know children who have gone off angrily to live away from their parents; and their mothers and fathers, again, wait in vain for some word from those children, word which will never come.

Every week I sit between a husband and wife who have lived together for years, their lives and their physical bodies have been joined in the most intimate kind of relationship. They have living children who bear in them the fruits of both of their minds and bodies. And yet, between them, there is no communication beyond mutual hatred and distrust.

Looking at this insanity, can we seriously question the existence of human sin? Can we question for one moment that we need help from beyond ourselves? Life becomes complicated in direct proportion to the number of people involved, and today about 85% of us live in our cities. Over one-half of the people in the United States live in our twelve largest cities.

The Bible narrative records that Cain, a murderer, built the first city, and he built it with all of the walls and the separations and the fences that exist today. And so the family lives eight inches away on the other side of the wall in the next apartment or a driveway-width away in the next house. And here we live, behind our fences, with no relationship and no sense of responsibility to each other.

One columnist tells of stopping at a fork in the streets of a strange city. He called out to one of the local citizens who happened to be standing on the curb: "Does it make any difference which of these two streets I take downtown?" "Not to me," was the reply.

Senator Hughes tells of eating in a restaurant in an eastern city. He had forgotten his watch, and he couldn't see a clock, and so he stopped a passing waitress and asked her what time it was. She snapped: "You'll have to ask your own waitress. This is not my station."

And so here we are, condemned to live closer and closer together, as the population of the world doubles in the next forty years. And we will keep building fences, and all of our fences will fail, because they will bring us only hatred, misery, and want and death.

The One whom we meet in this worship service is the greatest fence destroyer of all times. Society tried to put a fence around Him, between Him and the publicans and sinners, but He sought them out anyway and associated with them and ate with them. They tried to put a racial fence between Him and the Samaritans, but He broke it down. He walked through Samaria. He talked to Samaritans and even asked favors of them. They tried to fence Him into the polite, ecclesiastical society of the city, but He went out beyond the wall of the city into the countryside, and He talked to the peasants.

Every man who sat at that first communion table had some kind of a fence around him, but He broke down that fence with His own body and blood and made them all one body.

It is a simple and yet profound truth that the only source of unity that we have with people in many parts of this earth is the Sacrament of Holy Communion. NAME ME ANY OTHER TIE that we have with them!

Occupying Japan, an enemy country, after World War II, it was only after we received Holy Communion with our enemies that we felt that we had any unity or any fellowship with them. It was only in a Service of Holy Communion in Moscow that I felt, for one moment, truly at home in the Soviet Union.

Let us try to leave our fences behind us. I don't know what yours are. I only know you have some. Leave them behind you. Our Lord doesn't want them at His table. As the Word tells us in the Epistle reading: "We are all one body, even as we are all called in one hope of our calling, one Lord, one faith, one baptism." Or, as St. Paul reminds us: "Forasmuch as we all eat of this one bread and drink of this one cup, so are we all one body in Him."

That is our prayer -- that around God's earth, we may become one body in the body of His Son.

She Didn't Understand

"And Mary said, 'My soul magnifies the Lord, and my spirit rejoices in God my Savior.' "

(Luke 1:46, 47 RSV)

*****

"When Jesus saw His mother and the disciples whom He loved standing near, He said to His mother, 'Woman, behold your son!' Then He said to the disciple, 'Behold your mother.' And from that hour the disciple took her to his own home."

It is tragic that I, personally, cannot read these words without sadness. The sadness is not sentimental sadness, provoking tears, because these are the last words of a son to his mother. The sadness comes not because these are words born in the midst of excruciating pain. Indeed, the sadness is not caused by the fact that these words are spoken in the saddest scene that has ever transpired upon the earth -- the crucifixion of our Lord and Saviour Jesus Christ.

This is a sadness born of bitterness and revulsion.

Mingled with it is a certain amount of righteous wrath. Here is a glaring example of how the Word of God can be literally raped by well-meaning but stupid men, how the minds of men can twist and distort the Eternal Word until it bears little or no resemblance to the original, how men, in corruptness of ideas, can change the Word to support their own heresy, how a portion of the Word can be ripped from its context and all surrounding passages ignored.

It is startling to realize that if you were sitting in many churches of Christendom and an exposition of this text, the Third Word from the Cross, were presented, these are some of the things you might hear, and most of this is direct quotation:

Mary, the Mother of God, is the Second Eve. As death came into the world through the first Eve, so life comes into the world through Mary. When Jesus from the Cross said: "Behold, thy mother," He was not speaking to John alone, but to all mankind. With these words, the Lord assured us that we had not only a Father in Heaven, but also a Mother, the Eternal Mother of all mankind. Through her, the Mother of the world, we are granted life. Through her, the Eternal Queen of Heaven, and her intercession with Christ, we may have salvation. She is a perfect creature, born sinless, died sinless, and ascended into heaven without dying, where she reigns as Queen of all saints and martyrs. All things are possible with Mary, if she is adored. She is the hope of those who despair of their sins. She brings children to the childless. She brings healing to the sick.

Not only should we worship her, but according to the Decree of the Second Council of Nicea, we should adore and worship statues, images and paintings of the Blessed Mother. To adore her image or statue is to adore her, for, indeed, the paintings that we have of her from whom all paintings have come, were not painted by human beings, but by the angels. There are at least twelve hundred of these miraculous paintings and images. Some speak, some bleed, some weep, some of these images have been solemnly crowned by cardinals and popes. They have power of healing, granting favors, answering prayers.

In Aachen, Germany, you may visit the place where the garment of the Virgin and the original swaddling clothes of the Baby Jesus are kept in constant adoration. Or, as the Catholic Encyclopedia tells us, if we will wear the scapular, the badge of the Holy Mother, on our body throughout our life and have it on us when we die, we will be preserved from Hell. We may rest assured that the powerful motherly intercession of Mary will prevail upon her Son that He might grant us the grace of conversion and preservation in the faith.

Perhaps you would like to be told how Mary died, for certainly the way Christ died is of relative unimportance. All the apostles gathered together. Christ appears, receives Mary's soul, and hands it to Michael, the archangel. He takes it into Mary's body into Heaven and unites it with her soul. Adam and Eve are there, also, worshiping Mary and begging her to free them from the bonds of death to which their sin has brought them.

You would be told to say ten Hail Mary's, "Hail Mary, full of grace," to one Lord's Prayer, which the Lord Jesus Christ gave you to pray.

We Americans should be particularly careful about our worship of Mary, for the church has appointed her as our special guardian. In the Marian Year, which is the 100th Anniversary of the year the Church declared Mary sinless, we should pray to her all the more, for by special arrangement of the Pope, we will get double time off in purgatory this year for everything we do to honor Mary.

Jesus Christ? Mary's Son? Where is He in all this? He is the righteous eternal judge. We dare not approach His holy throne. He who said: "Come unto me."

Hear the words of St. Bernard of Clairvaux: "Dost thou not fear the divine Majesty in the Son? Wilt thou find an advocate before Him? Flee to Mary. In her, humanity is pure. The Son will listen to the Mother, and the Father to the Son." All this in the face of the admission in the Catholic Encyclopedia: "No proof of this dogma can be found in Scripture." All this in the face of the fact that Peter, supposedly the first Pope, said not one word about Mary.

St. Paul, the first great theologian of the Church and recorder of most of the theology of the New Testament, said not one word about Mary, though he did say: "There is ONE mediator between man and God, the man, Christ Jesus. Though early church fathers said nothing about Mary, though the early church services contained nothing about the worship of Mary, in spite of this, the church has chosen to place Jesus Christ, true God, in the position of having as His only claim to fame the fact that He was the only Son of the Virgin Mary. This is only a smattering. We have not sought to be extravagant in this. These things are mild in comparison to some statements that we might have read. I do not think that we are extravagant when we say, categorically, that this is the damned work of the devil. No such desecration of the eternal truth of God's Holy Word could be anything less.

My heart cannot fail to cry out in sympathy for our brethren within the Roman tradition who are in real danger of having the Gospel of Jesus Christ, our Lord and Saviour, stolen from them by a heretical, lunatic cult.

Fortunately, the Marian Cult lost out completely in the great Council of Vatican II, in my own opinion chiefly through the good influences of John the 23rd. Ever since that time, we have been able to note a continuing decrease in the emphasis of Marian adoration. The rosary, which is, of course, largely a prayer to Mary, has been less practiced and decentralized in worship. In attending Roman services today, you will scarcely ever see a worshiper ignoring what is going on in the chancel and instead "saying his beads." The rosary is not used as a form of penance so regularly. It is my opinion that, instinctively, our Roman brethren realize that if ecumenicity is to continue, then Marianism must be de-emphasized. Also, Roman Catholics are becoming more acquainted with the Scriptures and realize how little the Scriptures have to say about anything that is in agreement with their previous practices in regard to the Virgin Mary.

BUT LET US RETURN AT LENGTH TO THE WORD OF GOD. Let us return to a young Hebrew peasant girl whom God had chosen to have the signal honor of being His handmaiden, the earthly instrument that would bring forth His incarnate Son. Surely the fact that she was chosen of God, the fact that she willingly responded, is to her eternal honor.

"Behold the handmaiden of the Lord, be it unto me according to Thy word." These words in their beautiful, devout simplicity, are so typical of the uncomplicated faith of a fifteen- or sixteen-year-old peasant girl.

What a bewildering life she had before her! We can see her clutching her miraculously-born child to her breast in fright, as the soldiers of Herod carry out their butchery. We can see her in the temple as the old Prophet Simon took the child in his arms and made his solemn prophecy: "This child is set for the fall and rising of many throughout Israel. Yea," he says to Mary, "a sword shall pierce through thine own soul, also."

There was the visit to the temple when Jesus was twelve, and He stayed behind. "His parents did not understand." Always that refrain, "She didn't under-stand." We can see that Jesus' home life was not as happy as it might have been, because of this misunder-standing. Remember when He said bitterly: "A prophet is without honor in his own country and in his own home"? Or again He said: "A man's foes shall be they of his own household."

Imagine how it must have been for Mary, when, little by little, Jesus had to point out that He was not an ordinary son with only duties in His home and to His family. Imagine how difficult it was for Mary to bear when she came with His brother, seeking to see Jesus. His disciples told Him: "Your mother and brothers are waiting to see you." He stretched out His hand to all of His disciples and said: "Behold, my mother and my brethren. For whosoever shall do the will of my Father in heaven, the same is my brother and sister and mother."

The first person recorded who tried to give special homage to Mary was rebuked. A woman cried out in the crowd: "Blessed is the womb that bore thee and the paps which thou hast sucked." He replied: "Yea, rather blessed are they who hear the Word of God and keep it."

No, Mary did not understand. We can be sure that, many times, her heart was twisted with grief at the strange action of this unusual Son, bringing disgrace upon the family in their own city.

Here is the honor that is due Mary. Her faith saw her through. She never understood her Son, but she never stopped loving Him. There are perhaps no more beautiful words than those "Standing by the cross of Jesus was His mother." Her Son was being executed as a criminal, but she was there. As we have said, these words are, indeed, eternal. Each was brief and to the point. Each had significance. There was no time and there was no strength for that which was nonessential. Notice this, that the mission of Jesus is for all the world. He meets first things first. His first word was for His murderers. A word of forgiveness. We cannot understand all that word implies. The second was for the miserable creature at His side. We cannot understand the word of hope that He gave. We know that, for the thief, time was short. Our Lord fulfilled his need.

Our Lord was about to leave this life in the flesh. The days of His humiliation as the Suffering Servant were over. It is as though, at this moment, He is ready to make His last gesture as a human. He makes His last will and testament. It is simple -- no goods, no real estate, no wealth -- just the clothes that were on His back. They were in the hands of the Roman crap shooters.

Only a brokenhearted mother. As ages go in the Orient, Mary was old. The lines of suffering and pain showed upon her face. We can almost see the features of our Lord soften as He looks down. "MARY HELP US"? NO! SHE needed help. All of His love flows out to this simple, faithful, servant of God. Beside her stands the one disciple who followed Him to the cross. John has come a long way, too, from a "Son of Thunder," now to this.

There is no need for a long sermon here. Love never needs long explanations. "Woman," -- not "mother," notice, her motherhood of Him was over this long time -- "behold thy son." And to the disciple: "Behold thy mother." That was all, that was all that was necessary. We can understand those words. With them, our Lord shares with us the last of the earthly trials which all of us must share, the heartrending parting in death. Here He, in a simple way, fulfills the Fourth Commandment as He had fulfilled all the Law. He had honored His mother in the last moment and, thus, had honored all motherhood through the ages. Three days later, she understood.

"My soul doth magnify the Lord; and my spirit hath rejoiced in God my Savior, for he Hath looked upon the low estate of His handmaiden." "He that is might has done for me great things. Holy is HIS name."

So You're Mad at God?

"So Moses and Aaron said to all the people of Israel, 'At evening you shall know that it was the Lord who brought you out of the land of Egypt, and in the morning you shall see the glory of the Lord, because he has heard your murmurings against the Lord. For what are we, that you murmur against us?' "

(Exodus 16:6 and 7 RSV)

*****

The Jewish comedian, Milt Gross, has a story that I think points up our subject precisely. Irving was breathing out his last gasps of breath in the hospital, reaching the terminus of what we delicately call a "terminal illness." He roused from his more or less comatos state and saw the rabbi standing beside him, and he said: "And vhy are you here, would you tell me, please?" And the rabbi said: "Irving, I have come to find out whether you have made your peace with God." "Made my peace with God? I vasn't aware we had quarreled."

If what Irving said was true, then certainly he was a

rare person, because the real truth is that all of us, at one time or another, quarrel with God. There isn't a person in this congregation who can honestly say that he has never been angry with God. You have distinguished company. Job, for instance. I'm always somewhat amused when we talk about the "patience of Job." Job had no patience at all. In fact, the entire Book of Job is mainly made up of Job's indictment against Almighty God for His injustice, His inconsideration, and His lack of compassion, because Job was ANGRY at God. The great heroes of the Church -- Paul, Augustine, Luther, Wesley, Knox -- they all cry out at one time or another in the words of the psalmist: "I will say unto God, 'Why have you forgotten me?' As with a sword in my bones, my enemies laugh at me while they cry, 'Where is your God?' " They are angry with God.

How typical of the children of Israel to murmur against Moses and Aaron with the assurance that they would have rather died in Egypt where they sat by their fleshpots, their bellies were full of bread, than to be free men. Moses reminds them that they are not ANGRY WITH HIM or murmuring against HIM, they were actually revolting against, angry with, and shouting epithets at the Lord, who had brought them out of slavery into freedom.

Or bring it down to last week when a fine, young, Christian woman from another parish said to me: "How much is a person supposed to take? I have always considered myself a faithful believing Christian" -- and I'm sure she is -- "but now I'm so disgusted I don't know whether I even believe in Christ." It turned out that her first husband, by whom she had borne three sons, turned out to be a psychotic sadist, who beat her up regularly, placing her in the hospital at least twice, because he loved her. Her second husband was a man of tenderness, gentility, consideration, in every way different from the first. There was only one problem -- he was a homosexual, and would have nothing to do with her sons. And now, at long last, she had fallen deeply in love with a man, and they had talked of marriage. He told her that he would be glad to marry her, if she would agree beforehand that she would not interfere with any of his activities, or in any way restrict his liberties, or in any way object to his goals or objectives in life, and she should not expect him to take any responsibility toward her three sons. This is typical of a time when even the most convinced Christian becomes angry with God, and SHE WAS!

But she had made a typical mistake. She gave it away when she asked: "I've taught my sons that if they followed the laws of God that they would always have a happy life. And now they look at me, and they feel that what I have taught them is all a lot of bunk." And then, through her tears, she said to me: "I know that Jesus never promised us a bed of roses in this world, but aren't we supposed to have SOME happiness?" And so the questions came, and the tragic part of it is that they go deeper than just the surface questions. We are REALLY asked: "IS THERE A GOD AT ALL, AND IF THERE IS, WHAT KIND OF GOD IS HE?"

I can answer very quickly and unequivocally that if He were the kind of God that many of these questions that I have heard imply He is, I wouldn't believe in Him, either. But there's a difference, you see, between the psalmist and Job and I, because, you see, I DO KNOW what God is like. I have seen Him in the person of Jesus Christ, and the tragedy is that, though many people profess to be Christian, they have never gotten beyond the Old Testament ideas and misunderstanding of the nature of God. The legalism of the Old Testament they can understand -- the ancient, outmoded idea and code of an eye for an eye and a tooth for a tooth. Without thinking through one thing at all, they ascribe to God things that they wouldn't THINK of doing themselves. They think of Him then as a cruel, implacable, vengeful, vindictive and hateful potentate, and they train their children to believe the same. Again and again, I hear well-meaning but uninformed and rather stupid parents tell their children: "If you are bad, God will punish you." That sounds like very pious and wise advice, doesn't it? But the fact is that we could tell them no greater LIE about God. Of course, the inevitable happens. The child takes a chance, does the forbidden act, and God doesn't punish him. And so God becomes, in his eyes, just another myth like the boogyman, or the fact that mamma is going to call a policeman. Or, if by some coincidence, some tragedy or pain comes to the child, even if it is completely unrelated to the act, then the child thinks that God IS punishing him and that God is just a vicious, vengeful monster. Either way, you see, the parent or teacher or relative or friend has made a travesty of Christian training and Christian discipline.

And so this damnable heresy persists through the generations, and when we are confronted by pain, calamity, disappointment or death, we instinctively react as one man put it to me in words: "If this is the way God treats us, then I say to Hell with Him!" And I agree with him! I agree with him, because if this is the way God DOES act, then He belongs in Hell, because He is not God at all but Satan in disguise.

Lord Loundsberry, a long time ago, put an entry in his daily diary. You know, years ago, men used to keep a diary or a journal of every day, and this one entry was typical. He wrote: "Today I learned that Almighty God, for reasons best known to Himself, has been pleased to burn down my country house in the County Durham." His lordship probably thought that he was writing a very pious paragraph, but he was perpetuating an unmitigated, sacrilegious LIE! God did NOT burn down his house!

I have heard it just recently: "Well, old Tricky Dicky found out that God finally catches up and punishes everybody, even if it's the President of the United States." Again, a pious-sounding lie! I suppose that

Almighty God set out two hundred years ago to set in motion a political system which, if misused and abused, COULD result in a tangle of corruption in which even the President of the nation would become entangled. I suppose that God brought into being Ehrlichman and Haldeman and Dean and all the rest, just to punish Richard Nixon. I suppose that God revealed to Edison the mystery of recording sound, which finally resulted in the tape recorder, which finally resulted in the resignation of our President, so that, in the end, we would all look with fear and penitence and say to ourselves: "This is what God does to us, if we are sinful." We had better watch it! God ARRANGED all this!

In other words, God is like a father, who puts his son's hand in a vice and then turns it and tightens it, crushing the son's hand, until finally the son screams out in his agony that he LOVES the father. If this is what God is like, then I repeat, "to Hell with Him!"

In Thomas Hardy's tragic novel, "Tess of the d'Ubervilles," the entire tragic story ends with this sentence: "And so the President of the Universe" -- what a horrible term for our Heavenly Father -- "And so the President of the Universe had finally finished his sport with Tess." That was the conclusion of the novel.

Studdert-Kennedy lashed out in these lines -- though he didn't believe them himself certainly, at those who thought that God had deliberately brought on the horrors of World War I to punish mankind for its sinfulness:

> "I hate the God of power on his hellish, heavenly throne,
> Looking down on rape and murder, hearing little children moan.
> Are there no tears in the heart of the eternal?
> Is there no pain to pierce the soul of God?
> Then He must be a fiend of Hell eternal,
> Beating the earth to pieces with His rod."

Does that sound irreligious? No more so than anyone

who looks at one of the tragedies of life and says: "This is God's will." YOU'RE A LIAR! "God took my little child." "God caused my child to die." "God wanted to punish me, so He made my business fail." "God brought on this drought and the world starvation that will accompany it, just to remind us who is still running this universe." EVERY STATEMENT LIKE THAT IS THE HEIGHT OF INFAMOUS BLASPHEMY, as the Christ of God clearly taught us. Christ taught us that when we talk like that, we are implying that WE are more loving, more just, and more compassionate parents to OUR children than God is to us, as a Father to us. If that isn't blasphemy, I don't know what is!

Let's remember this: God did not bring sin into the world. God could not create that which was in opposition to His own holy nature. God did not create sin. Man did. God does not cause death. WE do, with the help of the whole human family. We are, finally I think, this year, getting that through our thick skulls, as we see right now, for instance, the inflation that is surrounding the world, that we realize that this inflation is not a national, but a worldwide problem, and that we can't cure inflation in the United States of America, unless it is cured in the other great nations of the world. No man is an island, and no nation is an island, as we used to like to think back a couple of generations ago.

We are one human family, and Paul reminds us: "If one member suffers, then all suffer together," but he also points out the other side of the coin: "If one member is honored, all rejoice together." Drop a pebble in the ocean, and the waves made by that pebble will wash the shores of every continent upon earth. One man's innocent little misdemeanor might create a chain of events in which MILLIONS suffer. The Bolshevist leaders, a few of them, nodded their heads and five million Ukrainian peasants were allowed to starve to death. Adolf Schicklgruber nodded his head, and six million Jews went to the gas chamber. Or make it close and personal: a father sins, and his child is born syphilitically blind.

Why did God create such a world? Because the only way we could be a human family is to serve each other and that, of course, also gave us the alternative of hurting each other. If we were denied that power, then we would not be human beings. Remember then that an American soldier, wounded in the Pacific in World War II, might have owed his life to the Japanese scientist, Kitasato, who isolated the bacilus of tetanus; a Russian soldier saved by a blood transfusion owes his life to an Austrian, Landsteiner; a German soldier is protected from typhoid fever by a Russian, Mechnikov; a Dutch Marine in the East Indies is protected from Malaria because of an Italian, Grassi; a Chinese is protected from infection by a Frenchman, Pasteur. Our children are guarded from smallpox by an Englishman, from rabies by a Frenchman, from diptheria by a Japanese and a German. So, whether we want to or not, God has made us into a family that will either serve or hurt each other.

You ask: "Why, then, doesn't a loving Father protect us from our own stupidity, mistakes and the results of our sin?" The answer is simple. God wanted children to LOVE, not puppets to manipulate, and so He had to give us the one thing that makes us human -- freedom of will, freedom of choice. It is our glory as human beings. It can, of course, also be our curse. We only know that, without it, we could not rightfully be called the sons of God.

Let me draw a parable. Years ago, I spent a wintery afternoon trying to teach our younger son to ice skate. I could have gone on holding him up, as he wanted me to in the first place, but I knew that if I continued to do that, he would never learn. And so, I had to turn him loose. One tooth-jarring fall after another followed. He was finally a whimpering little boy. His clothes were wet and cold. His seat was sore. His ankles were tired. And he was hungry. But I could only say with apparent indifference and even cruelty: "Come on, now, get up and try it again, or you'll never learn. I took a hundred times that many flops before I learned to skate." But before an hour had passed, the lad was stumbling unsurely along beside me, and he was smiling and calling up to me: "Look, Daddy, I can almost keep up with you!"

Fellowship with the Father! Yes, God limits himself, but He did not leave us alone. There was only one way He could help men without limiting their freedom, and that was to become one of them, to share their lives, to show them by suffering for sins which He never committed, what could really happen. They could bring on the horror of the Cross on Calvary. And even then, you remember, the Father did not intervene. Man was allowed to carry his sin throughout its horrible course and extract its terrible toll. But, while man had his evil day, God had His third day, which was the story of forgiveness, life and eternity. THAT IS WHAT GOD IS LIKE!

Want to Imitate God?

"Therefore be imitators of God, as beloved children. And walk in love, as Christ loved us and gave himself up for us, a fragrant offering and sacrifice to God."

(Ephesians 5:1 and 2 RSV)

*****

Not long ago the daily press carried a story that was certainly not news to any of us. Dr. Marvin A. Block, the Chairman of the American Medical Association's Committee on Alcoholism, said that "People are drinking more today as a very necessary adjunct to conversation." He concluded his statement on the subject with these words: "People can't stand each other as people any more." Well the question is obvious. If people can't stand each other as people, how can they stand each other at all?

The other day I heard a teenager put our all-too-common attitude in rather blunt but, nevertheless, descriptive, language. He was speaking of someone, and he said: "He's a creep. He gurgles my insides. He makes me want to puke." Yes, we feel it and, sometimes, if we are as candid as teenagers, we even say it. We make each other sick -- and we do.

I was recently looking at an astrology book that someone gave me. It's the only truthful astrology book that I have ever seen. It is entitled: "Why on Earth Were You Born?" and the subtitle that says: "The astrology book that really socks it to all those horrible, nasty people you don't like."

Here are some excerpts in which it describes the people born under the various signs: "Aries people are tops in everything. They are the absolute most! The pushiest, the nerviest, the most overbearing and arrogant, the bossiest, the most egotistical, etc.

"Taurus people may not sound too exciting, but they do have a lot of interests like eating, sleeping, reproducing, breathing, sitting down, lying around, scratching themselves and dozing off.

"If at some future time some person tries to tell you that Cancer people are miserable drips, cornballs, milksops, plainjanes, or insipid creeps, just remember that you read it here first.

"All Leos are typical: stuck-up, pompous, ostentatious, dictatorial, boastful, exhibitionistic, madly in love with themselves.

"All that any Virgo wants to be is happy. The trouble is that they can't really be happy unless they have something to bitch about. These people's sole mission in life is to point out what's wrong with the world.

"Pisces is the last sign of the zodiac, and it serves them right. These poor fish are born losers. Their sign is two achovies swimming in opposite directions, and they'll probably end up on a pizza."

Well, that's a sample. That's what we really think of each other. There's not one of us, I don't think, who has not been convinced, at one time or another recently, that nothing would be so satisfying as living life as a hermit. A single look at our world would reveal the tragic number of fragmentary groups and individuals. All the while, in typical, psychological jargon, we babble about integration -- integration of society, integration of races, integration of the family, integration of personality -- and even as we babble, the splits get wider and the number of pieces become more numerous. Often we say that this is a "crazy" world, and we are literally right, if we take the original meaning of the word "crazy." It comes from the French word, "ecraze," which means split up, broken, shattered. And just so, we have the Chinese Communists and Chinese Nationalists. We have Russian Communists and Chinese Communists, East Germans and West Germans. We have Jewish Palestinians and Arabian Palestinians. We have Moslem Indians and Hindu Indians. We have Nationalist French and Algerian French. We have Turkish Cypriots and Greek Cypriots. We have pro-Western Lebanese and pro-Eastern Lebanese. We have North Vietnamese and South Vietnamese. We have Northern Americans and Southern Americans. We have Eastern Americans and Western Americans. We have rural Iowans and urban Iowans.

When I was contemplating coming to St. John's as pastor, a man who had lived here in this city for several years said to me: "Des Moines? That isn't a city, it's a group of neighbors at war with each other. Everytime someone in Des Moines gets a $10 a week raise, it puts them in a different class, a different neighborhood, and a different political party." How ecraze can we become?

Human life today is caught between two contending currents; on the one side, the unifying forces creating proximity; and on the other hand, the disruptive forces preventing community. So there is our stabbing and ever-present problem -- proximity without community. One Irishman said recently of the bloody struggle between the Protestants and Catholics in Northern Ireland: "It's too bad that all Irishmen are not atheists. Then they could live together as Christians."

We look out this morning on a world that is sick with hatred; and yet, that hatred is an individual sickness. Cities cannot hate. Nations cannot hate. Political ideologies cannot hate each other. The world is sick with hatred because individuals are sick with it. That we can see on every side. We see hatred in our homes, families torn and mutilated by it. Do you have any idea what a devastating experience it is for a pastor to, again and again, be confronted by husbands and wives who share the same house, who sleep in the same bed, who together have produced the same children; and yet, they hate each other? Recently, the husband of a divorced couple told me how he and his wife were trading their children back and forth. And he told me almost proudly: "When I have them, I give them everything and spoil them silly, and it really bugs my wife when she gets them back and can't control them." Well, you have to hate pretty strongly to do that sort of thing.

Our social lives are permeated with hatred. Recently one of our college girls dropped out of her sorority at school because she couldn't stand the hypocrisy of the girls calling each other "sister," when they really felt the way they did about each other. Our business and professional institutions are saturated with hatred. One man told me that the only way to get ahead in his firm was to stab in the back everyone who was ahead of you. We see hatred organized -- the Ku Klux Klan, for instance. Is there any more monstrous blasphemy than to hide a hating heart beneath the white cloth of purity and the cross of love?

What is the answer to hatred? Well, certainly not diplomacy, not antidefamation, not racial tolerance -- what a horrible word, tolerance -- not social engineering, and not education. We have brilliant haters, clever devils all through our society. No, dear friends. The word is LOVE. Now, that's a nice, weak, effeminate, ineffectual word, isn't it?

But just wait a moment before you close your ears.

We might define love in a myriad of ways, but I would like to call your attention to a simple, yet profound statement. In the 5th Chapter of St. Paul's Letter to the Galatians: "Bear one another's burdens and so fulfill the law of Christ." What is that law of Christ? Those of you who are interested in preserving the law, in establishing the law, in keeping a government of laws instead of men, listen to the LAW! Strangely enough, it doesn't have anything to do with NOT lying, NOT stealing, NOT engaging in illicit sex, NOT drinking, NOT murdering. The law of Christ doesn't have anything to do with NOT doing something. Our Lord Jesus Christ puts it plainly: "Love is the fulfilling of the whole law." The law is love, and love is the law.

In another place, He says: "A NEW COMMAND-MENT I give you" -- please notice that Jesus isn't offering a suggestion or presenting to us an option -- "A NEW COMMANDMENT I give you that you love one another even as your Heavenly Father loves you." Essentially, the love of which Christ speaks is a life outgoing in sacrifice -- outgoing to God, outgoing to man. So Paul gives us this simple, practical, understandable system for developing this outgoing life and, thus, fulfilling the law of Christ: "Bear one another's burdens." Here in psychological language is the transformation of the EGOcentric life into the CONcentric life, the life pointed inward to the life pointed outward. Bearing one another's burdens is just that -- carrying another's load, identifying yourself with him, walking in his shoes, endeavoring, vicariously, as much as possible, to experience what he experiences.

Perhaps the great disease of our age is egocentricity, our apparent inability to shake ourselves loose from ourselves. An almost unbelievable preponderance of our mental, nervous, and physical ills are due to this self-centeredness. The egocentric person is a thin-skinned person. He goes around with a proverbial chip on his shoulder. He's not only waiting for someone to offend him, he is subconsciously HOPING that someone will. The next time you meet him (and that won't be long), stop and analyze. When I am confronted with a childish display of his temper, what do I do? I have two courses of action. One is to display temper of my own and, thus, assert my self-importance over against his, my self-centeredness against his, my ego against his; or, I can bear his burden. I can put myself in his place. I can understand that he is a sensitive person because he's a frightened person. He's unsure of himself. He's unsure in this world. He's being hateful, paradoxically, because he wants to be loved, and he's not sure that he is. If I let my life flow out to him in love, his need is answered. He has no more use for his fear or his temper. I have known many men that could never be defeated in open combat, but in thirty years of the ministry, I have never met a man who could not, finally, be overcome by love.

Actually, we find that this is the secret of the great lives that we have known about us and in history. Lincoln, for example. Some of those who treated Lincoln with the most hatred, contempt and spitefulness were some of those who were supposed to be closest to him. Stanton was always doing something mean and nasty and petty behind his back. McClellan, the Commander of the Army, publically insulted the President. And yet, Lincoln never took revenge in any way, as it is done in the highest circles today. He declared once that he would wipe McClellan's boots, if only McClellan would find a way to end the war and bring peace again to the nation.

On the other side of the Mason-Dixon Line, General Robert E. Lee was once asked his opinion of a Confederate officer, and he gave the man an unqualified commendation. He told how much he thought of him. His interrogator asked: "Do you know what he says about you?" Lee replied: "You asked my opinion of him, not his opinion of me." BIG men! Yes, that's what it takes, big, masculine men. It takes big men to love.

Booker T. Washington, the great Negro leader,

understood. He said -- and what a motto this is for human life: "I resolve that I shall never allow a man to narrow or degrade my soul by making me hate him." Hate does not destroy the one who is hated -- it destroys the one who hates!

We are greatly concerned about world starvation, but there is no more threatening starvation than the world's hunger for love. Carl Rogers, one of the nation's foremost psychotherapists, has described the healing of his patients as a movement toward "belonging." He writes: "The client moves from the experiencing of himself as unworthy, unacceptable, and unloved to the realization that he is accepted and respected and loved." And then he becomes well. A baby is born with the need to love and be loved. Its first contacts with tenderness and warmth or, on the other hand, with rejection, will leave lasting marks on that child. When our love-needs are thwarted, our growth is retarded.

For example, we are told of an orphanage in South America where there were about 97 children in residence. They ranged in age from three months to three years. They were just tiny children. The home was a lovely, comfortable place. The rooms were pleasant, the food was good, and the staff was above average for that type of institution. There was only one catch. There were ten of these tiny children for each member of the staff. As one doctor said: "All the staff could do was to see to the physical needs of the children. Opportunities for emotional interchanges were few, and any development of warmth or love between the worker and the children was impossible." The doctor continues: "At the end of three months, I noticed that the children were crying more than normal children of that age. At the end of five months, the smallest children began to refuse to eat their food. At seven months, the children's facial expressions in repose became almost grotesque. And after a year, 21 out of the 97 children had died -- FROM LACK OF LOVE! No other diagnosis was possible. This is not just an old wive's tale or a sentimental story. This is scientific, observable, clinical fact.

The world is hungry for love. Look at the person sitting next to you, maybe husband or wife, maybe friend or child or mother or father. That person that you will meet tomorrow, your neighbor, your business associate, if he seems to hate you or be your enemy, it's paradoxically because he wants you to love him, and he's afraid that he's not acceptable. He's afraid that the world does not love him, and so he's frightened and insecure.

You're interested in law and order? Well, here it is. There can be no order without law. And here is the law, the fulfilling of the whole law, not some Elsie Dinsmore, sentimentalized, impractical idea. This is not something that Jesus Christ said would be nice, if we were good, little children and did. This is the LAW! "I COMMAND YOU TO LOVE ONE ANOTHER." That means you, my friend, and you, and you. It means that you are to love every mother's son and daughter with whom you have any contact. It doesn't ask you to decide whether he's worthy of your love, or whether he's ready for your love, or whether he'll appreciate your love. Did God ask that about you, before He gave you His love? The law of Christ says: "Love him." And how we need that law in our world!

I remember the story which Dr. Mordecai Johnson, the Negro educator, tells of a colleague of his. He tried to interest his friend in Christ, win him for the Church, but he was always met by polite evasions and refusals. Finally Johnson pinned the man down to tell his story. It seems that when he was growing up in a little southern town, an evangelist came to that town for a revival, and the boy was drawn to the big tent where there was all the excitement. Each night, he had crawled back to one of the chairs that was reserved for black people in the back of the tent, and as the meetings came to a close at the end of the week, it was announced that the climax would be on Sunday morning when all of those who were ready to receive Christ would be baptized at the river. Those who wanted to be baptized were to appear there dressed in white. So the boy hurried home and told his mother what he wanted to do, for he was strangely drawn. At his request, his mother took a sheet off of one of the beds and fashioned him a little white robe. Proudly, happily, and somewhat frightened, he made his way to the river bank on Sunday morning. Oh, it was quite a crowd and quite a service, quite a celebration. There was a great deal of hymn singing and praying and Scripture reading. And, one by one, the candidates were led out into the river and baptized into the church of Jesus Christ, the King of love. And finally, the service and all of the celebrating was over and everyone had been baptized, and the crowd dispersed . . . all except one -- a little black boy dressed in a white robe who stood alone on the river bank, still waiting, because nobody had noticed him, nobody had talked to him, nobody had baptized him.

He's still standing there. His face is many colors. He comes in many sizes and many ages, and he's in many places. And he's still standing there, a thousand million of him, begging us: "Please fulfill the law of Christ. Please love me."

"Therefore be imitators of God, as beloved children. And walk in love, as Christ loved us and gave himself up for us, a fragrant offering and sacrifice to God."